MW00936442

To Laurie,
Keep up the good
fight! With my
best wishes,
Geo Walsh

A Fallen Marionette

I Was A Prisoner Inside My Own Body

GEO WALSH

A Fallen Marionette
I Was A Prisoner Inside My Own Body

ISBN 978-1-72381-556-0

To Jonah

Preface

This narrative is the true story of my journey through ten months of continuous hospitalization due to a rare illness caused by a ubiquitous bacteria. The statements attributed to all caregivers are based on my best recollection and understanding of events as they unfolded. The accuracy of the timeline is grounded on my own memories, discussions with my wife and daughter who were with me on most days, a journal they kept, and hospital records including physician notes. In addition, I undertook extensive online research to ensure all information regarding the disease is correct. If there are any errors, I am certain they are minor and will not negate the core facts of the story. It is my sincere hope that every reader, whether a professional in the medical field or a lay person, will find this account of my ordeal interesting and personally beneficial as well.

To see a World in a Grain of Sand
And a Heaven in a Wild Flower,
Hold Infinity in the palm of your hand
And Eternity in an hour.

~ William Blake

Part One

I was like a fallen marionette tossed aside by a thoughtless child. With legs twisted, arms tangled, head bent back, mouth gaping, I lay in a pile of disjointed pieces tumbled against the rail of a hospital bed.

They had positioned me sitting upright for the pre-dawn X-ray, but when the young technicians pulled the imaging plate from behind my back they flipped me over. I had landed sharply against the bed rail, which was cutting into my emaciated ribs. My upper body was hanging over the rail, wrenching my neck and spine. I was uncovered except for the patient gown, and the chill in the room was penetrating my bones. They began packing up; they were going to leave me like this.

"God. Poor guy," one said.

The other answered, "Yeah, I hope I never get that bad."

I wanted to scream, "I can hear you!"

But I could not scream though my mouth was wide open. I could not close it, speak, nor swallow. I could not draw a breath with which to scream. I could not move a hand or finger to signal them. I could not open my eyes to see them.

But I could still hear, so I listened, waiting for the sounds of someone coming to help. I strained to catch any approaching noise in the corridor – usually wheels, a footfall perhaps – becoming louder and then stopping, and my door opening.

Then I will sense a change in the air pressure, hear a soothing voice. I'll feel strong hands easing me to the center of the bed, unfolding my arms and legs, laying me out. Soft blankets will descend on me, and warmth will grow inside me.

I was calm but I was not brave. I was given drugs that numbed my mind, making my emotions as still as my body that morning. I wasn't afraid. I wasn't angry. I wasn't even sad.

I reflected on how ironic it was that a few days earlier I was swept into the center of a drama that was all about me – yet I had the smallest role. I was the star of this show but at the same time only a spectator, or a prop.

I'm at the mercy of strangers to keep me alive. My body has completely shut down. But inside my mind I'm fully conscious and aware of everything around me.

This is what it's like to be totally paralyzed, I thought.

As I lay there with each painful moment pressing on my mind the curious nature of my existence, I wondered:

Will I ever get better?

My supervisor appeared in the department doorway. My body tensed.

"George, Kaitlin and I would like to see you in HR," she said. It was a little after noon on October 2, 2012.

"Sure thing, Cora." I had been fearing this for weeks. I knew what was about to happen, but tested the water. I motioned toward the pad and pencil on my desk.

"Will I need to take notes?"

Cora's bland smile twitched a bit on one side of her mouth; she knew I knew. "No need," she said flatly.

"Alright. After you." I followed her across the deserted field of cubicles to the Human Resources manager's office. Everybody else was at lunch, but I was asked to stay and prepare some reports for a VP's meeting that got "pushed up." I knew then my time there was done.

What seemed a golden opportunity eighteen months ago had turned into a nightmare. I got in on the ground floor of a start-up division in a larger, established firm, where we were to do direct mail and online marketing for outside clients as well as the owner's existing companies. My boss was an exceptional salesman and marketer who could really bring in business. Unfortunately, he was disorganized and tended to overpromise on deadlines.

The entire division was just him and me, and I was experienced in client relations, copywriting, graphic design and managing production. It was fun and the business took off.

I thought it was the perfect blend of stability and growth opportunity, and that it also might be my last chance to have a secure and satisfying job so late in my career. Finding work had been getting tougher for years; I was fifty-seven when I got this job. I felt lucky to be there. I couldn't have been happier.

The good times ended at the start of the new year when the owner put a lot more internal work on us, about doubling our workload. To make sure our baby would not fail, my boss and I started working sixteen-hour and longer days, seven days a week, for over three months. He was a textbook workaholic and always took on too much. I think it was this added stress that led to his burnout, which caused him to make a critical mistake. That error set the most important internal program behind six months and severely hurt sales. He was let go and our division was dissolved.

I thought it might still work out. Citing my flexible skills and experience, I put myself forward to become the head of the new, scaled-down department handling the internal work. Instead, they hired Cora, a woman half my age. I knew my duties would become mostly administrative and, since I was being paid too much for that role, getting rid of me was an easy way to cut the budget. Yet I was in denial, making myself believe I could remain valuable by working hard to fix the backlog, and hoped to just keep my job after that. It was my priority, and believed it my purpose, to help my family.

Unconsciously, however, I must have known it was going to end badly because the feeling I tried to ignore – the fear over losing my job – manifested itself physically. It was the very first Saturday after the new manager started, in mid-April, when I felt a particular and familiar pain under my right ribs. It was sharp, deep, and lasting; I knew I was in trouble. That same pain in that place had already been the harbinger of several serious health crises, hospitalizations, and even surgeries.

What was the problem? My old enemy, myself. Literally – because I have an auto-immune disease, one of a spectrum of inflammatory maladies that includes multiple sclerosis, rheumatoid arthritis, lupus, and others. These are all chronic conditions in which your immune system goes haywire and decides a healthy part of you is a problem that must be destroyed. My flavor is Crohn's disease, which primarily affects the intestines. It causes inflammation, ulcerations, abscesses, and can be fatal. Before this flare, at one time or another I was prescribed probably every drug available to control it and had four surgeries dating back to 1975.

For a few months I kept it under control with a steroid, but you can only take those on a short-term basis. In the meantime, my work duties became more menial. I was assigned new tasks with no notice and minimal training, while the inevitable corrections and criticism became more and more demeaning. The growing stress from this exacerbated my Crohn's; as the job got worse so did my health. I got small, sharp pains in my upper abdomen after eating almost any solid food and began to lose weight.

I searched desperately for another position, but there was nowhere to go. One day, I promised my late father not to quit, to work until retirement – or as long as I was able – even in a hellish job, to do my duty to my family like he did. I wondered how long I could hide being so sick, and whether one day I'd just keel over and be carried out by the paramedics. That would be a big topic around the water cooler that afternoon, I imagined.

That afternoon would never come. Today was my last day.

"Please sit down," Kaitlin said, gesturing to the far side of the small conference table. I'm sure the professionally pleasant smiles on the two women's faces matched my own. No need to make this more horrible than it is.

I sat down onto a loose and wobbly seat; the chair was broken. If I landed any harder, I'd have fallen headlong against the far wall. I caught myself but needed to balance carefully to sit. *I can manage for a while; this won't take long.* It also seemed appropriate to be sitting in that broken chair, to feel like I was on a bubble about to pop, because in minutes I'd be out of work in a very tough market at the ancient age of fifty-eight. I worried about maintaining insurance coverage and if I could afford the co-pays for the next step in trying to control my illness. In the meantime, I nodded along with the boilerplate Cora was intoning across the table.

". . . and since he has decided to reorganize the marketing function comprehensively and prioritize his new internal initiatives, I'm afraid . . ."

You're afraid? It must feel great to be your age.

". . . we're going to have to let you go. I'm sorry."

Then Kaitlin took over with the paperwork, asking me to initial this and sign here, and handed over my last paycheck, crisp and hand-signed. I cleaned out my desk, packed up the family photos, and left. None of my co-workers of eighteen months were there to see me go. When I got to the lobby the receptionist wasn't there either. I walked out unnoticed, disappearing silently like a ghost.

"**W**ell, your Crohn's is still progressing, George. We need to get a handle on this now, before it gets worse."

I was sitting in an exam room of my long-time gastro-intestinal doctor a week after my dismissal and had just updated him on my symptoms. By then Doctor Sinha had been my primary doctor for over fifteen years. Sitting hunched forward on the rolling exam chair, he wore a look of concern but spoke with encouragement.

"I want to prescribe a new medication that has shown very good results, a biologic. As it is manufactured with a newer process it should not cause the allergic reaction you had in the past. In some cases, it has not only halted the disease process, but enabled the patient to achieve remission. I think it's the best choice for you now."

"Well, Doctor, I'm willing to do whatever you suggest. I've been thinking another biologic was the next step, since I responded so well before. I'm anxious to start. I can hardly eat any more. Will this be an infusion, like the other drug?"

"No. It is a monthly shot. It is sent to your home and a nurse comes to administer it. I need to point out there is an increased risk of infection with these drugs. You will need to be very careful while you are getting it. Use a lot of hand sanitizer. Do not get a flu shot."

"I understand," I replied. "I'll be careful. But okay, let's do it. Things keep getting worse down there. It's going to be impossible to find work if I get any sicker."

Dr. Sinha nodded, and said, "Good. I'll send the order in this afternoon."

In all those years I had been his patient, every therapy he prescribed had always been quickly approved, including very advanced medicines like this new biologic. We expected to begin the treatment within two to three weeks. With good reason: anyone prescribed this medication needs it, and it also may help the patient avoid surgery, which is even more costly and much more dangerous. It seemed an easy decision for the insurance company; by saving both the patient and money, approving the medicine would be a "win-win."

With those expectations, it felt like a slap in the face when I opened the letter denying treatment. My breath got short and I panicked for a moment, thinking, *What's going to happen to me?*

"Not medically necessary," the letter read. That didn't make sense. My doctor says it's necessary; isn't it his decision? And now it's even more necessary because my condition had worsened in the four weeks since the order was put in.

Dr. Sinha may have been even more upset than me. A few days later in early November, he excused himself during an appointment to call the insurance company about this. I could hear him through the walls, shouting over the phone, berating the utilization department person about the denial. "He is wasting away in front of me! What am I supposed to tell my patient?"

They replied they would review his appeal and get back to us. I just had to wait; they didn't say how long. In the meantime, I was getting no therapy at all for a severe yet quite treatable condition.

While I waited for the new medicine, the calendar and my illness advanced in tandem. By mid-month I was having repeating sharp pains across my upper abdomen. In early December they became more intense, more widespread, longer lasting. The week before Christmas the first obstruction occurred, when a portion of my intestine became inflamed and swollen to the point it closed off. My abdomen was so tight it hurt to sip water. I could not eat anything.

Soon the obstructions were coming every third to fourth day. Each lasted for up to two days during which I couldn't do anything except wait for the obstruction to ease. I would only get relief when the pressure forced me to start vomiting, followed by diarrhea. My eating became sporadic, and I lost weight more quickly.

As the frequency of these episodes was rising, so were my frustration and anger, because the medicine being held back from me was supposed to have prevented all this in the first place. It was not until mid-December when I got the authorization to begin the medication – but it wouldn't start for another month, almost ninety days after my doctor's original order. By then three months of pain had passed. So much damage had been done. I wondered what the repercussions would be of their denial and delay.

My worry and anger faded once I got the first shot. Within

two days my pain decreased significantly. I felt excited and relieved. The medicine was having a powerfully positive effect, just as I hoped.

Biologic drugs are used to treat a range of auto-immune diseases such as Crohn's. They work by suppressing your immune system so it stops attacking healthy tissue; unfortunately, biologics have the dangerous potential side effect of increasing the risk of infection.

I took precautions but soon developed a strange respiratory infection. I had quite a high fever, but all my other symptoms were unusually slight. In fact, both catching the infection and my body's strange reaction were results of the drug suppressing my immune system. Antibiotics quickly cleared up the respiratory infection, but an even worse problem was brought to light when I opened my big mouth.

"Well, the infection is gone," the doctor said, "so you may continue with the biologic with no interruption."

"Great," I replied, "I think it's really working. There's a spot on my lower right abdomen that's itchy and feels hot, so I think it must be doing a lot of work there."

The doctor looked worried. "Let's take a look at that, shall we?"

I pulled up my shirt and lay down. He felt the area I pointed to. The skin was bright red; it wasn't so red when I last saw it that morning. He pressed down, frowning. I felt his fingers detect a mass under the skin.

"I think you have another problem, George." He spoke

deliberately. "You may have an abscess there. I am going to order a stat CT scan tomorrow morning for you. When you are there, I want you to wait for the radiologist. If she does confirm it is an abscess, I want you to go straight to the ER. I will have you admitted immediately."

My eyes popped open. "Wow. Well, uh, okay. I'm glad I mentioned it. I think." I was dismayed. This meant another delay on my medication; you can't take a biologic when you have an active infection. Nevertheless, I was glad my doctor was acting so quickly to deal with this dangerous situation. I knew how bad it could become.

After the CT scan, the radiologist confirmed Dr. Sinha's suspicions. I started walking down the block to the hospital. On the way I stopped at my wife's medical offices across the street from the hospital, where she works as a diagnostic ultrasound tech, to drop off my car keys with a note about where it was parked and where I was going. It was a strange feeling to suddenly have to abandon my life, drop everything, and step into the unknown.

At the hospital it was the height of flu season and the ER was packed. With my compromised immune system and an active infection already raging inside me, I decided to wait outside while they got a room ready. It was a damp and windy day, but I couldn't risk catching something else from the people inside.

I was there for eight days, receiving intravenous antibiotics. The abscess subsided, but on the skin above it, a pustule formed that had to be lanced. The wound had trouble healing in the weeks ahead, foreshadowing another problem.

It was clear the insurance company's initial denial had set in motion a cascade of problems. First, the delay allowed the Crohn's to develop and grow worse, allowing an infection to develop. Secondly, since I got the medication after contracting the infection, its immune-suppressive action let the infection flare into a life-threatening abscess.

Those two factors set up the next problem. The infection took another six weeks to clear, during which I could not take the medication at all. When I finally did resume, it did not work half as well as it did after the first shot. The doctor explained that because I was exposed to the medication but then paused it, my body had time to develop a resistance to it. The medicine that offered such promise, and for which I had been so desperate, was almost useless.

All this preyed on my mind one Friday evening in early April. I was trying to rest in the recliner while repeating waves of pain washed across me. These by now were a constant in my life, agonizing jolts that shot across my belly in different directions. Everything seemed so mixed up inside there, so sick. It was at that moment when something different grabbed my attention.

I noticed a new ache, a slow cramping deep in my lower right abdomen, along with a crawling, itchy feeling at the still-unhealed wound on my skin. Then in horror I felt intestinal gas pass out of me at that spot. I could hear a hiss. It was unmistakable. The inflammation and abscess in my belly had eaten a hole right through several different layers of my living tissue to make a tunnel out to my skin. One's digestive tract usually has two holes, one entrance and one exit. I now had three.

Like the alien in the movie that hatches inside a man and bursts out, something within me with a will of its own had broken through to the outside world. It was a fistula, an unnatural passageway from the intestine to the skin or to an organ, or between sections of intestine. I realized that some of my food might leak out before I could absorb all of whatever meager nutrients I still could with a diseased gut. Or – worse to contemplate – my obstructions and cramps might force fecal material to back up and spill out, uncontrolled.

My disgust over this new development compounded my fears and frustration. I had been sick for a year, out of work six months, and we hadn't even slowed down the progress of my Crohn's.

For a while the fistula did not leak much, and not every day, and I was able to contain it with normal bandages. I was still hoping the medication had enough power to heal it. For a few weeks I thought I stabilized, and I believed I had turned the tide. This is how my mind began to work, in its growing but still subconscious desperation: every pause in the downward spiral I took as the turning point on my way to getting well. It was silly, magical thinking, but it sustained me.

I was not getting well; I was not getting better. Another very serious obstruction, the most painful and debilitating yet, put me back in the hospital in the middle of May. I was doubled up in pain and almost immobilized when I was admitted.

Their first thought was I needed emergency surgery, but Dr. Sinha and the top GI surgeon there decided to wait in case the obstruction eased on its own. If that happened, I could avoid an operation.

Trying to relieve the pressure inside me and buy time, they inserted a nasal-gastric suction tube, or NG tube. They began by poking it into my nostril, feeding it through my sinuses, and then pushing it down the back of my throat into my esophagus to my stomach. While it advanced, my eyes watered profusely and I swallowed madly to ease its way. Then they looped a piece of tape around it and secured it to my nose. The other end was connected to the suction pump.

An NG tube is invasive and uncomfortable; it can make the back of your throat quite sore. You always feel it pressing against the tender tissue. I am sort of an expert on these; this was about my fifth or sixth. I was able to tell the nurses my left nostril is the more accommodating, which made it easier – for them.

Besides the NG tube, since I was NPO because of the obstruction – not allowed anything by mouth – I also had an intravenous or IV line for hydration and medications. The bags of fluid and the pump are placed on a rolling pole, the bags hanging from hooks at the top, and since the IV line was connected to me, I was connected to the IV pole.

Late in my stay, Dr. Sinha thought I was improving and ordered a series of upper GI X-rays to take a look. So that I could leave the room for the exam, my NG tube was disconnected from the suction pump; the loose coil of tubing was looped and left dangling from the top of the IV pole. During the study, the technician pumped a contrast agent into my stomach and intestines through the nasal tube, took his pictures, and then removed the liquid – but not all of it.

After I returned to the room in a wheelchair, I first sat on the side of the bed. Because my symptoms had eased, the nurse didn't think it necessary to immediately reattach my NG suction tube to the pump.

It was the first time in over a week I was free to move around the room. There was a comfy-looking armchair by the window so I decided to go take in the view.

I felt dizzy as soon as I stood up. I stopped moving, grabbed the IV pole to steady myself, and tried to breathe deeply to get past the nausea. But then, without warning, my intestines cramped and an evil-looking gray-brown slurry of liquid feces mixed with X-ray fluid started pouring down my bare legs onto the floor. I hurried to the bathroom, walking through the mess in stocking feet. At the bathroom door I turned around and bent over, my bottom toward the toilet, pulling the IV pole along after me.

As I rushed in, the hanging loop of NG tube got hooked on the door handle, suddenly yanking it about halfway out of me, tearing the tape off my nose. I found myself sitting there on the toilet, the door wide open, everything covered with filth, wincing in pain, and my eyes bugging out at the sight of the stained, partially-exposed NG tube with the tape that had anchored it to my nose dangling several inches from my face.

What do I do? Should I push it back in? Is it contaminated now? Are my hands clean? Should I pull it out – but they'll only put another one in? But – this mess . . . .

I have never been more disgusted with myself than at that moment, or more embarrassed. I didn't want them to see what I had become, but I had to pull the call cord for help.

It is at a moment like this when you move beyond feeling sorry for yourself and believe you have become a burden to others.

"**U**nfortunately, George, I think you've come to an impasse. In spite of the severity of your illness, surgery may not help."

I was meeting with Doctor Nguyen, the top colorectal surgeon at that hospital, the week after my release. He consulted during my recent flare and operated on me several years earlier. I trusted him completely. I considered him a man of great skill, intellect, and compassion, and appreciated his willingness to answer all my questions. What does he mean, surgery may not help? Especially coming from such a good surgeon. If he can't help, who can?

"I don't understand, Doctor," I replied. "That seems to be my last resort."

He grimaced, his hands folded on his desk. "If you have surgery, you will lose some portion of your bowel. Since some unknown length of bowel was removed in your two previous resections, there is a strong possibility you won't have enough intestine remaining to absorb sufficient nutrients to live on. You would then need permanent intravenous feeding through a peripherally inserted central catheter, or picc line, for the rest of your life. It's a large IV that extends into a vein near the heart. Which creates its own problems. The picc line is like an open passageway into your cardiac cavity, creating a continual risk of quite serious infection.

"Finally, the feeding is a continuous 24-hour process. You have to carry a bag of nutrition and a pump everywhere you go. That will restrict your mobility and lifestyle.

"My point is, as far as your lifestyle is concerned, you might not be better off after surgery than you are right now."

I was dismayed. My first thought was, *Who is going to hire me like that?* My eyes widened; I held out my hands. "Then what is the option?"

"To live with it."

I knew Dr. Nguyen was telling me the unvarnished truth. I walked away from our meeting shaking my head. I worried I had no good outcome to look forward to. I felt disheartened to think that as badly as I felt right then – it might be as good as I'll ever feel again.

In the meantime, the continuing decline of my health and our finances put a strain between me and my wife. My unemployment benefits had expired, and she was shouldering the entire load in a stressful job. I dreaded the days she was off, hoping she'd leave me alone in my office and just go watch TV. But she always looked in at some point and the indoor fireworks began.

"So, how's the job search going? What is that? What are you reading, some political blog crap? What the – you know, I work all the time . . ."

"I check like five job sites every day, and get email alerts . . ." I cut in.

". . . fifty, sixty hours a week . . ." Her hands clenched. The hair stood up on my neck.

"I send out five, six resumes a week but there's no response. They just . . ." I hunched forward, feeling diminished, holding out my palms.

". . . while I'm paying all the bills!" She began waving her arms.

"Well . . . of course I want to . . ." I sputtered.

"It's just that I can't believe how cavalier you are about the whole thing!" Her voice was shrill.

I winced. "Cavalier!? How can you say that? You think I want this, and this isn't tearing me apart?" I couldn't breathe for a moment. "I can't possibly want a job more."

Her tone turned disdainful. "You are such a disappointment."

I had no defense for that; if I've disappointed her, how can I refute it?

"Well, at least we agree on something!" I yelled.

She shouted right back, "There's got to be work out there! Target! Walmart! You're not even trying! My job can be hell sometimes and you've been skating by on my hard work for all these years."

This stung deeply, but I knew I didn't need this added to the agony I already felt. I thought, *I can't let her make this worse. I have to push this away.*

As I looked up into her eyes, it occurred to me her anger was just another manifestation of this disease. She was hurting too. So, in order to not get mired in toxic emotions and bring on more pain, I silently said, *I forgive you.*

Her attack continued. "... and you don't even care!"

I shook my head. "No! C'mon! You know that's not –"

Her eyes narrowed. "What a – loser!" she spat.

I never knew words could be so sharp, and I had no shield. "Loser" hit me like an arrow; my guts tightened, shooting a jolt of pain under my ribs. She threw up her hands and walked away.

"I forgive you," I whispered.

I wasn't trying to be a martyr. I said it out loud to formalize in my mind the decision I had already made. Then, if anger and resentment ever surfaced within me, I could put it all aside as already dealt with, already settled. I was fighting for my survival and needed to stay focused on the big picture.

I almost felt I was fooling myself into thinking this way, but deep inside I knew I wasn't. Because I believed – even at the most difficult moments when I looked into angry eyes I hardly recognized – that she would be there for me when I need her most. No question. When I saw her from this perspective, forgiveness was easy.

In the weeks ahead, the fistula worsened; it was leaking almost all the time, and the fluid changed from yellow to brown. I was spending hundreds of dollars each month on bandages and coverings to contain the discharge. No adhesive could hold up against acidic intestinal fluids and each type of bandage failed at some point. I was constantly dealing with a gross, unsanitary mess.

To get some control over this, in early August Dr. Sinha sent me to the hospital ostomy clinic where I was fitted with a bag. It was sad to admit the fistula was not going to heal on its own. This solution was not cheaper, but the ostomy bags at least gave me some control within this nightmare.

To sustain me during the lengthening siege I started on liquid nutrition, TPN for Total Parenteral Nutrition, through a picc line into my arm and chest just as the surgeon had described. Each afternoon I strapped a day's bag of opaque white fluid into a small satchel and replaced the batteries on a pump, which over the next twenty-four hours pushed the feed directly into my bloodstream. It became my umbilical cord and my anchor, further limiting my mobility, although I had no interest in going anywhere.

Despite our frustrations, my gastroenterologist was not giving up on me. To try to find some way out of this, Dr. Sinha pushed the insurance company to give me a referral to the IBD clinic at Cedars-Sinai in Los Angeles for a consultation. Cedars' IBD clinic is world-renowned, and we hoped they could either help me themselves – taking me as a particularly interesting case – or tell us who could.

The doctor at Cedars wore thick, dark-rimmed glasses and his eyes blinked in a random pattern like they were reacting to his inner thoughts. I summarized my history, and I had already sent him copies of my scans and radiologists' reports so he was informed of the clinical situation.

"I'm sorry we don't have any clinical trials of any 'miracle drug,' as you put it, Mr. Walsh, appropriate for your advanced disease. Even if that were the case, you definitely need surgery."

I had expected that. Still, it was a heavy burden, to know for certain I'd have to go through a major surgery again – with no assurance it would make an improvement.

"But what about the other doctor's opinion that I could lose too much bowel and need liquid nutrition forever?"

The doctor frowned even more, but the corners of his mouth turned up – was that a smile? He leaned back in the high leather chair and blinked several times. He spoke slowly, as if letting me in on a little secret.

"It is possible that could be avoided if you have the right surgeon," he said. My ears perked up. "There are two here in Southern California who specialize in Crohn's you might see."

I blew out a breath. This was the first good news in a year.

I knew the first doctor. He had operated on me eight years earlier at Cedars. He was very good but didn't take insurance.

"The second is Doctor Miles at UC Irvine Medical Center; they have a new digestive diseases clinic there where he practices. He is a pioneer in new techniques to save as much bowel as possible, which may give you a better outcome." He leaned forward and folded his hands on the desk, still giving me that odd, nervous looking smile but his eyebrows shot up. He blinked twice.

This seemed too good to be true. UCI Medical Center is only thirty minutes from my home in Orange County, while Cedars is two hours away or more. I also knew a medical center teaching hospital will be exhaustive in requesting tests and diagnostic imaging. The doctor himself is on the leading edge of surgical technique. In addition, since it was also the county hospital, I knew the medical center accepted our insurance.

I knew I had to see this doctor, and felt like I just found the trap door to escape this maze of misery. As soon as I got home, I checked the provider network listings and saw that while the hospital was in my HMO network, the doctor was only in their PPO network. That meant I needed their approval to go out of network and get the care I desperately needed. A simple formality, or so I thought.

You probably can guess what they said, and by that point in this saga I also should have expected it, but I was still stunned when I got the rejection letter from the insurance company. This decision did not make any sense – again. First, they decide to delay the biologic medication so I got sicker to the point where I'm hospitalized twice. Then, because I'm terribly sick, they approve a consultation with one of the world's leading clinics in my disease to get some direction on how to help me. But when that doctor provides that direction, and says I need the skill and expertise of a particular surgeon, they ignore his advice. That's twice, when the path to getting well was right in front of me and the way ahead was clear, the insurance company made exactly the wrong decision and denied me the proper care.

In recent years, I've heard of many patients negatively impacted by increased premiums, higher deductibles, and narrowed provider networks, but I didn't believe it would happen to me. It was infuriating, frightening, and such a change from my past experience. I wondered, *Are they through with me? Have I been enough trouble over the years and now they're cutting me off? Am I just a statistic in their ledger book?*

I believe that was exactly the case. I think the decision to delay the medication until January was made to cut costs, to put me into the next year's budget. Eight months later, I was paying the price of their short-term thinking, physically and emotionally.

$\mathbf{T}$his latest denial drove me deeper into despondency. About ten days after getting that letter, it happened to be my birthday, the big five-nine. It was a Sunday and I was alone; earlier I had dropped my wife off at the pier for a walk.

Sunshine streamed through the bedroom window, but I was in a black mood. Pain and disappointment plunged me into profound gloom. My worries over current problems widened in scope to encompass my entire life and the prospect of an ignoble end to it. *So this is where I've come to on my birthday,* I thought. *What do you have to say for yourself?*

As I think everybody does occasionally, I started talking to myself inside my mind. My inner voice was cold and insinuating, and it said:

Well, Geo, it's just the two of us; you can stop lying. No need for your ridiculous magical thinking that everything's going to work out if you just believe it will.

Face it, you're not going to get better, and even if you do survive, you'll never be healthy enough to work again or ever be useful for your family. And looking back, you never provided for them like you should have, although you could have. You must not have tried hard enough. So many of your friends have done so well, but you – you simply wasted all of that so-called talent and intelligence you were oh so proud of. What kind of man is that?

So, between us, why not just go ahead and admit what a total failure you are? You know, when you add it all up. And here's the proof: your own body is killing itself because it knows what a failure you are. It's killing itself – how stupid is that! Talk about a failure – in fact, you're a biological mistake that never should have happened. You never should have lived.

But you egoistically made it all worse by having a family. You helped bring them into this world, and then you failed them, so they are worse off for the very life you gave them. Another level of failure!

Look at yourself – see the irrefutable ironclad logic of your complete and utter failure. Look what you've done to your family – why don't you stop hurting them? Why don't you just die?

The world, the room, my mind fell silent. I felt still . . . and for a long moment I came to believe the ultimate falsehood regarding any human being: that in the vast cosmic scheme of things it does not and will not matter in the least if I had never existed at all, no more than if one single grain of sand in all the world were to disappear.

And then in a flash a plan came to me how I could correct nature's mistake. I had everything needed right there on the property. Painless, no mess. Then, if that idea was a flash of lightning, it was followed by a double thunderclap.

The first reverberation was a feeling of overwhelming shame to have even thought of such a thing as taking my own life. It hit me like a blow to the chest; I felt exposed to the world as utterly selfish and ungrateful to everyone who ever cared about me, to life itself. I could not hold back my tears.

I never felt so reproached and so low, yet I think it was this feeling that saved me. Rather, it was a sign of some remaining well of pride inside myself, a last reservoir of belief that I still had value on my own terms, which allowed me to still feel shame. It wasn't clear to me at the time, but I must have believed, down deep, I did deserve to live, and that I should keep fighting.

The second thunderclap was a sense of empowerment. In spite of the shame there was also clarity. I realized I still maintained some measure of control over events, and I needn't be at the mercy of the insurance company and the Crohn's that were conspiring to kill me. I didn't have to wait passively for that degrading and pitiless end. If I didn't win this thing, at least I can choose when to lose it.

And with this understanding, my train of thought stopped. Like a cloud, it evaporated.

A thought occurred to me; it seemed funny: *I can't kill myself today, my wife needs a ride home a little later.* I got out of bed. I decided to go outside and enjoy the warm summer day.

In this encroaching darkness, one spark of hope remained. The open enrollment period for the medical insurance was coming up, so I had one last chance to change the trajectory of my healthcare by getting out of this dead-end HMO bureaucratic labyrinth. It put a significant strain on our finances, but we upgraded to the PPO so I could see the surgeon I needed to see. It was a matter of life or death.

November came, and the new plan took effect. The very first day, I called the university clinic and was astounded they could see me the following week. The once-locked gates had swung open.

I arrived to my consultation wearing a baggy, untucked flannel shirt and jeans now much too big, my belt cinched to a new hole I put in to make it smaller. I was exhausted after the short walk from the parking structure. I slumped into a side chair in the exam room, staring at the opposite wall. My entire middle was in pain; it was hard to concentrate. Beside me was the satchel with the bag of TPN and the pump pushing it through the picc line that ran up under my shirt, down one sleeve, and into my arm – the trickle of electricity barely keeping the bulb inside me flickering.

My lethargic state was broken when Dr. Miles burst into the room. He projected an air of great self-possession. He was young, about thirty-five I guessed, with piercing clear eyes and a spike of blond hair. *The rock star surgeon,* I thought. He smiled and shook my bony hand.

"Mr. Walsh, good to meet you. We've seen your studies." He held up the two disks of scans I sent the clinic. He sat down and waved his hand at me. "Please, tell me your history," he said eagerly.

I filled him in on the timeline, the worsening symptoms, and my concern about losing too much of my intestines. I concluded saying, ". . . which brings me to you, Doctor. I'm hoping you can get me a better outcome."

As I told my tale of woe, he was staring at me, nodding frequently, leaning forward on the little rolling chair, a little fidgety but never breaking eye contact. While I spoke, he didn't act worried or sorry for my suffering. He was obviously engrossed and absorbing it all, and I believed he wanted to help; he just didn't act daunted by how bad of shape I was in.

Another patient might be put off by this manner, but I needed a doctor, not a counselor. His demeanor was unexpected but intriguing, and I started thinking he could fix this, and I could get better. He had the confidence of a visitor from a happier future.

When I stopped, he nodded his head, keeping the same assured smile, his eyes still locked on mine. He lifted his eyebrows and shrugged.

"Well, you definitely need surgery, so let's schedule this."

I laughed, surprised my life-saving procedure was suddenly a reality, and at his matter-of-fact attitude toward performing surgery other doctors were reluctant to tackle. I thought, *My disease has finally met its match. I present a difficult problem and this genius wants to solve it.* I also considered that in his vigor and fearlessness he was like a great athlete, the all-star player who wants the ball at crunch time, who loves the toughest challenge and was born to meet it.

I felt liberated. I was in the right hands at last. The strategy to switch to the PPO to gain better access to healthcare providers of my choice, and pursue a better outcome, seemed to be succeeding. I felt hope for the first time since becoming ill. After the glacial pace of care during the previous eighteen months, everything shifted into overdrive.

Then the big day came. In pre-dawn darkness we drove up to the gleaming new facility, welcomed by the warm glow of the soaring lobby. I was nervous about the outcome because you never know what the surgeon will find and I had been so sick for so long. I was aware this could be the miracle I've been waiting for – or I may not wake up.

For the next eight hours, the surgical team undertook a very complex and delicate procedure to confront my advanced illness. Dr. Miles later said the challenge he faced in handling and repairing such severely diseased tissue was "like peeling apart a wet newspaper without tearing the pages." The post-op report reads like a horror story written in clinical terminology, noting multiple fistulae, several abscesses, and some portions of irreparable tissue removed. As part of his plan, Dr. Miles also gave me an ileostomy to allow the latter portion of small bowel and colon to rest and heal, which was to be closed six weeks later.

When I woke up in recovery a nurse said, "You did fine, Mr. Walsh." Like I did anything. All I did was sleep inside the car while they worked on the motor.

By the time I got home a week later, I was giddy with gratitude for my new lease on life. I savored the sweet freedom of being pain-free, of moving around the house or going to the store unchained from the picc line and nutrition pump. I still wore an ostomy bag, although in a new place, but I was accustomed to that by now and knew it was temporary.

The single greatest pleasure, however – other than simply surviving, of course – was being able to eat solid food again. With better nutrition I got a healthier color, was in a better mood, gained a little weight. Since getting sick I had lost sixty-five pounds, almost one-third of my original weight.

After being a walking science project for so long, the second operation to reverse the ileostomy was routine. I was relieved when everything worked normally and overjoyed I didn't have any extra holes in me for the first time since the fistula broke through more than eleven months earlier. I was hospitalized less than a week when they said I could go home. The next morning my son came for me, and they rolled me downstairs.

Outside the hospital door, the car was waiting at the curb. I stood up from the wheelchair and stepped into the sunshine.

Part Two

$\mathbf{F}$rom that brief walk in the sun until the first sign of another and even more threatening disease was just two weeks. And from that moment I had only two days to live.

The first symptom was a small thing, but already the final countdown was well underway. Inside me a force was building that would sweep through my life like a tsunami. The disease that struck me is unexpected, it sneaks up and strikes quickly, so the blow is more surely going to be fatal. By the time the symptoms began, I was deep into a fight for my life against a danger even greater than the one I had just survived.

It is difficult to write this part of the story because I become overwhelmed by strong emotions, and they've only surfaced since I sit here and try to explain myself. As the memories flood in I feel terrified, grateful, and relieved. I experience wonder, sorrow, and joy. Tears well up and my throat tightens. I need to step away.

It is also hard to relay even the plain facts because I feel so emotionally distant from the person I was. I feel sympathy, but also anger – anger born of frustration because I can't change the past. I want to reach back and shake myself, to yell, "Tell them what you have! Tell them what's going to happen!" But that person in the past will always only experience events as they unfold.

It was a warm spring morning, Tuesday, March 25, 2014.

When I awoke, I noted it was two weeks since I was discharged home after my grueling two-year battle with Crohn's. My joy at renewed health and hope was in full bloom; the sky was a brilliant blue since dawn.

I slept well, had a good appetite, the intestines moved as expected. It was exciting how well they were working since the surgery that made my bowel intact. When you have Crohn's, this can be a big deal any time, but it was a wonder considering how extensive and comprehensive my illness was. I made myself breakfast. I shaved and showered, got dressed. I went back to work on updating my résumé and trying to figure out how to explain why I was off the last eighteen months. I wondered if "taking care of a family member during a health crisis" could fly. At least it was true.

A small dark cloud appeared on the horizon around mid-morning. The new normal was I'd have a second bowel movement around that time, but it didn't happen. I was quite concerned, being hyper sensitive to every nuance of its function. Nothing changed in my diet or schedule, and I felt fine. Something wasn't right.

My concern grew when just before noon I developed a stomach ache. It was a general tightness under my ribs, where I felt the worst of my recent pain. It was similar to the early stage of an obstruction, yet more widespread, but I knew I'd have to be very sick for many months to reach that distressed state again.

In the early afternoon, about four hours after the first anomaly, things got weird. I was sitting in the family room. I think I had my head down, and then I lifted it while I looked up toward the front window – and the world slipped apart into two separate images.

It was double vision, but not like when you cross your eyes on purpose to make a funny face. When you do that, your eyes stay level and the images slide across each other sideways. What I saw had about the usual overlap of normal vision, but one image was higher and one lower. Also, the eyes didn't move together as a pair; one lagged behind the other, making everything swim around, out of control. While my brain tried to focus on one thing in one of the visions, the same thing in the other vision floated around on its own, demanding full attention as well. My head spun. The world suddenly seemed unreal – if only it were true.

My first thoughts were, *This is new. This never happened. It's wrong; your eyes can't do this.* It threw me off balance when I tried to stand up, so I plopped back down. I decided I must be tired because I'm still recovering, or maybe I have a bug, or I need a nap. I just wanted it gone. Even though I knew this was a meaningful sign or symptom, I didn't want to consider it was serious or dangerous. I must have been in denial or had "illness fatigue" after the long fight with Crohn's.

I lay back in the recliner and quickly fell asleep. That was another anomaly. I hadn't needed a nap in several days and was feeling the strength and drive returning just as it did after earlier treatments or surgeries. I was surprised to awaken two hours later; it felt like minutes and I hadn't stirred. I still had double vision.

I got up, holding a hand over one eye, and went outside. It was a nice day, but I didn't care. I was angry but did not analyze what was happening to me or do any research about the symptoms. I merely stared at the two worlds in front of me, hoping this was going to resolve itself. My stomach still hurt; I had no appetite but sipped some water. While the double vision was a radical and bizarre thing, I was still more worried about my intestines.

In the evening I tried to watch television, covering one eye. My wife came home from work after her typical 12-hour day, made herself some dinner, and watched television in the spare room. We didn't say much. Around nine o'clock I was feeling tired and decided to get to bed early.

That was when another flag warning of the approaching storm went up. Holding on to the door frame because I felt unsteady, I told my wife I wasn't feeling well and needed to go to bed. Well, I said something that sounded like that. The words came out slurred; I tried it again and felt my tongue was thick and slow. She was concerned, but I wasn't very worried. I still believed this was all caused by a profound exhaustion from my struggle with Crohn's. I did feel more run-down that evening than I had been, which seemed to confirm my thinking – but it was another symptom.

My wife was up and out early for work; I slept in a bit and the morning brought no improvement. I wasn't hungry, my guts hurt, and the disorienting double world still flew around me every time I moved my eyes or turned my head. I just sat in the recliner looking at the floor. If I had to move, I walked along the walls or counters for support, holding a hand over one eye. That helped me avoid dizziness, but without the depth perception of true stereo vision it wasn't easy. It was certainly no solution to the underlying problem, whatever it was. My speech was still slurred; it was worse than the night before.

If left to my own devices at that point, I would have continued playing the waiting game. It is a game I would not have won.

My wife and I have two grown children, boy-girl twins, then in their late 20s. At that time our son was living with us, and was home that day. He recognized I had a serious problem. He called his sister to discuss it, and she urged him to get me to the hospital ER right away. I took a quick, careful shower, and dressed slowly. Attempting to function with such severe double vision was like being on a narcotic or underwater. Try putting on pants that way: which right foot goes in which right leg, and why won't they both stop moving?

As we left, I said goodbye to our two dogs, thinking I'd see them later that day.

When we got to the ER, my son had them bring out a wheelchair and I was taken inside the hospital. The sleek professional interior and purposeful hum were very familiar to me; I was back in the system. Everything looked so rational and clean – the soothing colors, polished neutral floor, warm woods – all designed to be so reassuring. I was not at all at ease, although more aggravated than alarmed, remembering I was hospitalized four times for more than forty days in the last thirteen months. With my double vision it was more alienating than comforting.

At the triage desk my son described my symptoms, and the admit nurse looked over at me.

"Did you ever have a stroke before?" he asked.

I replied, "Well, I don't know if I've had a stroke now."

He smirked as if to say, "Okay, Pops."

Wrist bands were fixed to my arm. One said "Fall Risk." One, "Allergies." One for name, date of birth, medical record number. I stared down at them. It felt like only yesterday I cut some of these off. I was bothered to be experiencing these little things again, but I was not afraid. I told myself they would diagnose and fix the problem quickly.

We were taken to one of the stations in the ER where I met Doctor Habibi, the physician on duty who took my case. Later my daughter joined us; I was proud both my kids were taking such proactive care of me. I wondered how many people are alone when they are in crisis and must call 911 for help, and how many will find they've waited too long and are unable to call?

We had to wait a few hours until they got me into the MRI to scan my brain, but I was found wanting. No stroke.

The doctor decided to admit me to keep an eye on me and do more tests tomorrow. I said good night to my children from the gurney; they had done all they could, for now. I felt disconnected as I was rolled away. You don't see what everyone else does, lying there when they move you along; you only see ceiling panels, the undersides of beams and doorways, exit signs, and light fixtures rolling up over your head like a scene in a movie, or a bad dream.

In the room, two people helped me into the bed; I was shaky and the double vision was almost blinding as the two blurry worlds swirled around me, uncontrolled. The nurse made sure

I was settled and pulled the side rail up. The abrupt thump and shake when it locked in place were disturbing; I never needed the bed rail before. I tried to not get upset; I told myself this was no big deal compared to what I'd just gone through. But it was a real shock to be stuck in a hospital bed again, much too soon and much too sick.

There was something more than the normal noises and distractions of a hospital at night that awakened me a little after two-thirty. I was tired but restless; I couldn't take in a full breath. I wondered if the recirculated hospital air was to blame, if it was too dry, or there was something in it to which I was allergic. I raised the head of the bed as far as it could go to make it easier to breathe. It helped a little, for a while, and I slept fitfully. The restricted feeling was worse by morning.

I told Dr. Habibi about this when he came on his rounds about nine. I could only talk in short, staccato bursts of breath.

"Hi, Doctor. I've having trouble, breathing since, about two-thirty. Feels like asthma. I had it when I was a kid. Tightness, empty feeling. Seems worse now. Very uncomfortable," I slurred.

He made a somewhat dismissive face, and said, "That is probably related to your Crohn's. Most likely you have an ileus, an obstruction, pushing up on the diaphragm and restricting its movement and your lung capacity. You said you were having intestinal discomfort before your double vision, correct?"

This upset me. "Yes, but I don't think I, have an obstruction so soon, after surgery. Had Crohn's forty years, and it never caused, breathing problems."

"Well, Mr. Walsh, I think that is a separate issue from our

greater concern, which is your vision and speech issues. I've ordered some tests for you this morning. They should shed more light on what's going on." He nodded with a reassuring smile and said goodbye.

As he walked out, I thought, *How different for me, for once in my life to not have a diagnosis.*

Soon after, they took me down for a spinal tap; no one told me what it was supposed to find.

Later in the morning I realized I needed to cancel an appointment the next day at the university medical center, since it was obvious I was not getting out of this hospital in time. By then my speech had deteriorated further; I could only speak well enough to explain it to the nursing assistant and ask her to make the call. That appointment was my first follow-up, and I was disappointed I wouldn't see my rock-star surgeon and make my triumphant return.

By noon, my breathing was worse, making me agitated as I tried to alleviate it. Once I stayed in one position for a while, my breathing got quite labored, which forced me to reposition myself to get relief. In a little while, this posture also grew so uncomfortable I needed to move again. I began to switch from sitting up on the side of the bed to lying down, then sitting up, then lying down, over and over. Each change helped, but only for a while. Then the squeezing feeling and breathlessness again became intolerable, and I once more had to change position. Ominously, each compelled change came sooner than the last. Back and forth, up and down I went, while minute by minute my time was running out.

It was about then I realized I could no longer speak. I could not make a sound, even grunt or squeak. I can't remember how I reacted to this. I understood this was a radical development, but did not immediately tell anyone. Perhaps I was too preoccupied with my breathing, or too stunned and afraid to do anything, or maybe the lack of air was causing me to make bad judgements.

It was the better part of an hour later when I decided I had to complain to the nurse, not due to my loss of speech but because my breathing was growing almost intolerable. I hoped they would give me oxygen until it improved. Since I couldn't talk, before I called for help I typed out the message on my mobile phone. It was difficult pressing the right keys. My coordination was failing, but I didn't connect that, or my immobilized tongue, with my breathing problem.

When the nurse came in, I pointed to my throat, waved my hands, made a worried face, and shook my head "no." I handed him my phone with the message: "Breathing worse. Now can't talk. What does the doctor say?"

He tilted his head and shrugged. "Yeah, well, we think it's an ileus putting pressure on your diaphragm, from your Crohn's."

I looked into his eyes and emphatically shook my head "no" to communicate they were on the wrong track. That didn't affect his attitude. He left without promising any further action, or that he'd tell the doctor I could no longer speak. I was annoyed but thought they might know best. After all, they were the professionals.

At this point, please reflect on this crucial fact: Since we did not know what I had, we didn't know I was in any danger; therefore, I was not monitored to automatically summon help in case of an emergency.

I was left on my own while my body was quitting on me, while I was straining to suck in every breath. Each shallower than the last. Each threatening to be my last.

I became too tired to move. I felt limp. I stared across the room at the wall clock. How sad, how brutally ironic – if nothing changed or happened right then, my last flicker of consciousness would have been the sight of the sweep hand on that clock ticking away the final seconds of my life.

Then Dr. Habibi walked in. I was surprised to see him. I didn't expect him until evening, if then, as only an hour ago the nurse was so offhand about my deteriorating condition.

"Hello, Mr. Walsh. I hear you're having more trouble," he said. He came around the bed and stood over me. "I understand your breathing is getting worse and you can no longer talk?"

I nodded. *Maybe he found what's wrong, and I'm going to get some help.*

"Can you sit on the side of the bed?" he asked. I scooted over carefully, dizzy from the double vision.

"Can you stick out your tongue?"

I could not. I shrugged my shoulders to let him know. That is, I tried to shrug –

The blackness descended over me.

I stopped breathing and collapsed unconscious.

With the M.D. standing over me. Talk about good timing.

When I blacked out, at that moment of destiny when I fell and the doctor caught me, he and I and the hospital team found ourselves in a race against time, and against death. I am very lucky it was a race at all; death thought this would be no contest. Its strategy was to sneak up undetected and strike with irresistible force, expecting to find me alone and undefended.

If death had its way, within sixty seconds my brain cells would become starved of oxygen and start to die off. By three minutes, the process is much advanced and, of course, irreversible. At the five-minute mark, brain damage is severe. If it stopped there I might still retain some shards of personality, at least inside my mind, but never regain normal physical function, perhaps losing speech and sight.

By ten minutes, my liver would begin to stress and malfunction. I could go into cardiac arrest and suffer instant death. At fifteen minutes I'd be dead or wishing I were, if I still held on to any cognitive function we recognize as human.

Were I alone when I collapsed, there is no way I could have avoided that. The next visitor would find me dead.

But – instead of imposing on me that lonely and pitiless

demise, rather than winning the race unopposed, in my case death did not even have a head start. Immediately after I passed out, my doctor called a Code Blue, the protocol for an emergency resuscitation announced over the PA system, and had the room's oxygen mask over my face.

At sixty seconds after passing out, rather than having brain cells burning out, I was already getting oxygen. Most of the medical team, including Dr. Habibi, nurses, nursing assistants, and respiratory therapists, was already on the scene, jumping into their roles. Dr. Habibi was the captain of this group of people who owed me nothing, yet who on my behalf brought remarkable skill, training, and compassion into my room that day.

The head of the bed was lowered, the bed pushed away from the wall, the headboard removed. It was confirmed I had to be intubated – have a breathing tube inserted into my trachea. The order was given.

The respiratory therapist, standing over me behind the bed, tilted my head back and opened my mouth. The RT inserted the laryngoscope, sort of a shiny crowbar with a light on the end, into my mouth and under my tongue, then lifted the tongue up out of the way to reveal my vocal cords. Holding the airway open, she or he – I don't know if it was a woman or man who did this amazing thing for me – inserted a tube down past the vocal cords into my trachea, used a syringe to inflate the cuff that holds the tube in place, and connected it to the oxygen supply. The intubation took about twenty seconds.

And with that, my life was saved.

My eyes opened to see the swimming double images of a blank wall. I was lying on my side and the bed rail was down. The room was spinning. My ears were ringing. I did not notice the tube in my throat.

I became aware of activity by my feet. I could only slowly look that way. There appeared to be sixteen, maybe twenty people in the room, everyone moving briskly, and two big red carts. The swirling doubled images seen sideways from the bed made it look like all these people were walking on the floor and the walls and floating up on the ceiling. They were busy.

It was like waking up after surgery or a procedure, but I realized whatever it was wasn't over yet. Everyone was still working, with a lot of that short, back-and-forth talk. My body was being jostled; I felt hands on me. It took a few seconds, but the pieces of this puzzle began to fall together: *I'm waking up, but I know there were no procedures planned so what am I waking up from, and why is this happening in the room, and why are there so many people in here? There must be –* In that instant I knew I was in mortal danger and was seized by an overwhelming terror.

They noticed I was awake.

"Good job, Mr. Walsh."

"Everything's fine, Mr. Walsh."

Those words, at that moment, were exactly what I needed. This was quick-acting medicine, bypassing my conscious mind to impact my fear directly. It took only microseconds to absorb it – "good job" means I'm past the danger or the worst of it, "everything's fine" means they've got it under control. I understood this was out of my hands, I must trust these busy people, and I could.

Their words took effect just in time, as I then slipped back into unconsciousness.

I had received sufficient oxygen in the first few moments after I was intubated to revive and awaken into the ongoing emergency, but just before an anesthetic I had been given took effect. Then I passed out again, protecting me from the trauma of seeing anything more than a glimpse of the disaster engulfing me and imprisoning my fully aware mind inside the paralyzed shell of my body.

Our most terrifying nightmares are, in reality, exaggerated reflections of our true fears, framed in a distorted mirror.

I was in a nightmare. It began with the awareness that I was in terrible pain over my entire body; I knew I must be badly injured. I was in darkness. I felt crunched into a ball and squeezed from all directions. The pressure and pain were so great I could not move any part of me. I must have fallen into some very deep narrow hole somewhere. I tried to remember the last place I was going – *Was I walking near construction?* – and a sudden panic swept over me that I must have fallen into a crack in the earth, and no one will ever look for me here. I've disappeared from sight, I was lost, hopeless. I was going to slowly die here.

I noticed a dim light far above me. In the light I could just make out the silhouettes of people looking over the edge of the pit. My heart leapt – I was not alone! They must have seen what happened. They know I'm here! They're calling down to me. I couldn't understand the words but they sounded like they want to help me.

I felt a glimmer of hope and as they spoke to me the light around me grew brighter until I was back in the moment. I knew I wasn't in a hole, I was in a hospital. I've been unconscious for a while. I was able to understand that the problem that brought me here had become worse, but I did not recall the problem.

The room seemed brightly lit but large areas of my vision were obscured. I could see my legs in the bed and the lower parts of two or three people working in the room who disappeared when they moved around. In a few more seconds my consciousness grew enough to take in a figure sitting to my right. I knew he was a doctor, but it was not Dr. Habibi. I could not look toward him, and his face was in the shadow blocking out the upper part of the room.

As he talked, I regained some awareness that there had been an emergency. I knew I had been in great danger, but it didn't upset me. I had no recollection of going through it or what it was; I was merely aware of the fact. He said they were working on the problem and moving me to a different room. When he stood up to leave, probably as a reflex after all my hospital experience, just trying to be a good patient, I gave him a weak thumbs-up.

He was pleased; this made me feel somewhat encouraged, thinking I must have exceeded his expectations. I thought he was glad I wasn't as bad as he thought, but perhaps he was happier I was just responsive. This was the first sign that whatever neutralized my body had not affected my brain, my consciousness was normal, and I – the real me, experiencing all this in real time – was still inside.

Soon I was alone and all was dark. My mind was a blank. I knew I was in the midst of a serious situation with my health and medical care, but I did not, I believe I could not, think of what just happened to me. I did not go over why I was in the hospital or the events leading to the crisis. I did not know I almost died, or that I survived only by the thinnest of margins, the most fortunate of coincidences. I knew I wasn't moving but not that I could not move. With all the drugs I was on, I did not recognize or even wonder what my physical problem was: I was paralyzed.

My wife found me in the Intensive Care Unit later that evening; I don't recall it. But when I awoke early the next morning, she was there, holding my hand, crying.

Dr. Habibi joined us mid-morning. My vision problem persisted and I could only see his lower body in the corner of my right eye. He probably examined me; I only recall he said something about my hand, asking if I can move it again. I tried to give him a thumbs-up, but my hand was weaker than the previous night. I sensed he was disappointed; I was. This was a sign the disease wasn't done with me yet. It was clear my paralysis was getting worse.

He told my wife he thought he knew what was affecting me.

"We believe he has Guillain-Barré syndrome. Guillain-Barré attacks the nerves and interferes with their function, causing loss of motor function, even paralysis. It usually begins as numbness and weakness in the legs and rises upward in the body over several weeks. But in about five percent of cases symptoms start in the eyes, as your husband's apparently did, and it can also progress quite rapidly and cause respiratory failure requiring mechanical ventilation.

"Guillain-Barré syndrome is also an auto-immune disease, and your husband has a history of Crohn's. So, even though his case is atypical, given these signs and his risk factors, that's the most likely diagnosis at this point," he said with an air of authority.

His tone changed and became more apologetic. "But it

has not been confirmed. The first test was negative. I'm sorry to subject George to that again, but we need to do another spinal tap to make sure." Quietly, almost questioning, he added, "They probably just didn't get enough fluid."

Despite the uncertainty, he had already ordered treatment for it, which was starting later that day to prevent the GBS from doing further damage. It was called plasmapheresis, a blood filtering process, and would take four hours a day for three days. I was relieved they had a plan but worried about how much the spinal tap would hurt.

By the evening after the second treatment, however, I knew Dr. Habibi's diagnosis was wrong. I must have heard him telling my wife that the second test was also negative, or they did not see some expected change or improvement. The cause of my paralysis remained a mystery.

It was early the very next morning when those young X-ray technicians came to take a chest X-ray and flipped me to the side, then abandoned me, in pain, uncovered, like a fallen marionette left tangled and tumbled against the bed rail. Their treatment of me was the most blatant demonstration yet of my vulnerability, and it provided clarity even in my numbed mind. I started to accept that my paralysis was not a temporary condition quickly cured, but must be the normal, lasting, perhaps permanent effect of – something so rare they can't even identify it, much less fix it.

This is what it's like to be totally paralyzed.

Lying there, cold and hurting, waiting in my medicated calm, listening for someone coming to help, I began to understand my new existence. This was the moment I first wondered:

Will I ever get better?

Suddenly I heard the sound of an automobile pulling up and stopping very close to me, right on the other side of the wall. It was bizarre I hadn't noticed anything like that in the two days I had been there; it was only a few feet away. It seemed to be inside the building. I realized the room or the ICU must be next to a parking lot or garage structure, and with someone arriving so early, it must be employee parking.

Yet, even odder than having a car almost in the room with me, after the driver got out and closed the door, he started whistling an extremely annoying little tune.

It began with the first part of a very familiar melody, although I can't remember it, like an advertising jingle, or the title chorus or melodic hook of a Beatles' or Beach Boys' hit – a catchy song you've heard a million times. But the second line wasn't the one you expect to hear, the icing on the cake; it didn't go at all with the first part but was more like a jazz riff or racetrack fanfare.

I thought, *How could this guy not know the second part of that melody? Everybody knows that tune. Is he trying to be creative? Is he a frustrated musician? Is it a joke?* It was such a random thing to intrude on my sad and sterile world.

The whistling faded as the driver walked away. A moment later I heard a heavy exterior door slamming not far from my room somewhere behind me. I knew it was not a lobby door or public entrance. I thought, *OK, that is definitely an employee parking lot out there. Now, wouldn't it be something if he works in the ICU, he's punching in now, and I'm his first patient?*

My tangled limbs and twisted joints ached with the hope this was true. The bed rail pressed sharply into my ribs. My body never felt such biting cold, yet I could not shiver.

The room, the hospital outside my door, all was quiet. Then from the hallway with growing volume came that inane and maddening whistling, that crazy pop tune turned inside out. It got louder, it was coming closer, it stopped outside my room. The door opened.

"Hi, I'm Rob, your respiratory – oh, look at you! Let me get you some help."

It was a mystery: there was no stroke, no GBS, no injury, no tumor – yet there I lay. Something had blown out the circuits, but no one knew what. And I didn't know if I would get even the least bit better.

The medical team cast a wider net and took more blood, ran more labs to find the cause of my paralysis. In the meantime, I was a mere bag of biological processes kept functional only by advanced technology and the continuous oversight of my care givers. I was living on the razor's edge of survival.

My memories of the next weeks are scattered and vague, as I was often adrift between sleep and a medicated twilight state. When awake, I knew how fraught and stressful the situation was; I was clear-minded and able to pay close attention to what people told me, others' conversations, and the activity around me; I was hyperaware of every sensory input: I felt movement, touch and temperature, and I could hear everything.

My left eye was closed since my Code Blue; the right eyelid stayed partially open at first but within a few days almost completely closed. Often it was bandaged to prevent injury, and then I was in total darkness. When it was uncovered, I could only see a dim arc of weak light low in my field of vision, on the periphery of sight. At times, the eye may have drifted open a little wider or my position was such that I could discern some color and form, a human shape, a hand holding mine, and I think I saw the plasmapheresis machine. I was never sure if any of it was real.

Surprisingly, what I could hear also let me "see." Those sounds prompted visions in my mind – people's faces, hallway traffic, the layout and colors of my room, the equipment in it – as if my eyes were wide open. A certain sound coming from a particular direction from a perceived distance would form one element of an imagined three-dimensional world I was constructing in my mind.

Emotionally, the only thing that sustained me in those days was having family present. My wife spent as much time as possible there but had her patients to see. My daughter, despite working full-time and living fifteen miles away, was there for many long hours.

My daughter was quite entertaining, dishing staff gossip after chatting with some of them in the hall, critiquing certain people's attitudes or bedside manner, and commenting on the care and medications in general. She was chatty, bubbly, and was capable of having a great conversation without any help.

She often made me want to laugh. One of the drugs they were giving me was propofol, a powerful anesthetic that works in seconds. My daughter noted that propofol was the preferred sleep-inducing drug of the late King of Pop. She knew that in my condition I welcomed the instant oblivion it provided, and one night teased, "Hey, Pops, I bet you're ready for your Michael Jackson juice!"

My wife's vigils were quieter. She would tell me news from the medical team, or how things were going at home, but often just sat with me and read the paper or a magazine. I liked when she was holding my hand, although I ached to squeeze back.

That Tuesday, a week after my symptoms appeared, was the first of April. I awoke that morning to the awareness she was there, but rather than sitting near the bed she was standing at my side. She was not just holding my hand but caressing it with both of hers with an insistent energy I never felt before. From her voice I knew she was upset. She spoke in a sobbing voice.

"Geo, please tell me this isn't really happening. It's April Fools Day, please open your eyes and tell me it's all a joke. Please, Geo, please." Her quiet crying filled the room and echoed in my heart.

"I was so scared when I came to your room that night," she continued. "The kids gave me your room number so I didn't need to talk to anyone at the nurses' station. So I didn't know anything. Then I came in the door and the room was empty – no bed, no Geo." She paused; I heard her suck in a breath.

Regaining strength but in a trembling voice, she said, "But there was a lot, a lot of trash all over the floor. Everywhere. All their supplies. They were in a hurry." I pictured the scene.

"I knew something big happened. Something bad." She began crying again. "And I wondered, 'Is he even alive?'"

I felt so bad for her. I thought of how I had disappointed her, and yet, after all that failure, this was even worse. Her career was the foundation of our family and here I was, not only no help, but a burden. I felt a pang, a fear that after all her hard work I would drag her down into poverty from the cost of all this. It was another epic fail on my part to dump it all on her, to quit on her.

So I was that much more amazed by what she said next. I will never forget her raw and anguished voice, and the tone of regret that tore at my heart.

"Oh, Geo, I'm, I'm so sorry for the way I treated you last year. I'm so sorry!" She broke down in tears.

I was stunned. After all the disappointment I caused, any kind of apology to me was the last thing I expected to hear from her. I was touched deeply. I wanted to say, *Baby, no, there's no need for that. You didn't mean it and maybe you couldn't help it. It's alright.*

It also occurred to me it was my getting sick that allowed this to happen. I don't mean this as if to say, oh sure, so now you're sorry – or that there was some tradeoff or I paid the price for this. I only thought, *Wow, there's a silver lining inside this catastrophe.*

At the same time, I realized it had to be enormously difficult just to bring the issue up. Even when we want to apologize and know it will do much good, it's embarrassing to come out and say the words. This took courage.

As her words echoed in my mind, a warm feeling coursed through my body, a sudden wave radiating from my chest of – I don't know, I just felt wonderful. It was a strange sensation, but I'm sure a doctor or scientist could provide a logical explanation for it. They might say it was caused by my brain sending out positive emotions, and the electrical surge overheated my nerves. Or, it was my blood pressure rising from being so happy. Whatever their opinion, I know what it really was.

I was loved.

What a precious gift. I was dumbfounded to receive such a transcendent offering amid this horror. I wanted to bask in its brilliance and let it bleach out the terror and sorrow. This is what I needed more than anything: Now I knew I wasn't going to face this by myself, because you're not alone when you are loved.

I wished I could reach up to touch her face, to open my eyes and look into hers, to breathe and speak of what this meant to me. But I just lay there, moved but unmoving, hearing only the ventilator's steady breaths and her quiet crying.

I didn't know what would happen to me, but I did know where she stood: at my bedside. It was going to be the two of us against – whatever may come.

Botulism: finally, the true diagnosis, confirmed by blood test. The word came that afternoon, one week after I first felt ill.

Botulism is caused by the toxin produced by the bacteria *Clostridium botulinum*. Botulinum toxin is widely regarded as the most lethal substance on earth, the world's most deadly poison. It is a neurotoxin, meaning it targets the nervous system, and therefore a very small amount can shut down your entire body. Inhaling as little as seventy *billionths* of a gram of the toxin will kill an adult human being. A researcher in Spain calculated that one gram of this toxin – about a quarter-teaspoon – is enough to kill 14,000 people if ingested, 1.25 million if inhaled.

I feel like it hit me like a tsunami, but the actual volume of toxin in my system the day I stopped breathing was quite small. Nevertheless, it overwhelmed my nerves as powerfully as a real tidal wave hits a beach. The way the toxin works is interesting but also frightening when I imagine – when I remember – it happening to me.

Inside the body, your nerves do not physically contact the muscle; there is a gap between the fiber-like tip of the nerve cell, called the axon, and the muscle fiber. When an electrical impulse comes to the nerve cell, the axon releases the chemical acetylcholine, which travels across the gap. When it reaches the muscle fiber, it triggers a chemical change that causes the fiber to contract and then some part of you moves. Whatever you want to do, you can't, if the release of acetylcholine is blocked.

That is precisely what the botulinum toxin does: it destroys the axon's ability to open the cell membrane, keeping the acetylcholine permanently sealed inside.

As the bacteria multiply and the volume of toxin rises, one by one, the axons can't do their job and, faster and faster, muscle fibers become inactive. Eventually enough axons go dead that an entire muscle stops. When the diaphragm stops, you die from respiratory arrest – unless your doctor walks into the room.

There is a fortunate paradox about botulism: although the spores of the bacteria are found commonly in everyday life including in soil, freshwater and saltwater sediments, household dust, even on the surfaces of many foods, very few people contract it. In the United States you are about twice as likely to be struck by lightning than to contract any form of botulism. According to the U.S. Centers for Disease Control and Prevention (CDC), there were 161 confirmed cases in 2014.

The large majority of those, 128 patients, had what is called infant botulism. It occurs when a baby ingests some *C. botulinum* spores, which are like the seeds of the bacteria. These spores find in the baby's intestines a hospitable environment where they are able to germinate into the bacteria that produce the toxin. The usual source of the spores is honey. It doesn't have to be wild or raw honey, just normal pasteurized grocery store honey, that cute little squeezable bear. Doesn't look like death, does it? But the next time you see a bottle of honey, notice the warning on the back: "Do not feed to infants under one year old."

Another type of botulism can generate national news: foodborne botulism. This usually occurs as an outbreak after several individuals at a community or family meal eat the same dish that was improperly prepared or stored, or from a home canning or preservative effort gone wrong. A lesser-known variety is wound botulism. All wound botulism patients that year were injection drug users. In the U.S. there were 15 cases of foodborne and 16 cases of wound botulism in 2014.

That leaves only two more cases that year, which means that out of a total population of about 320 million people in this country, the odds of catching botulism by any way other than infant, foodborne, or wound are about 160 million to one.

I was that one.

My case is categorized in the *CDC Botulism Annual Survey 2014* as "Unknown or other." I must say that's a rather underwhelming phrase for something that landed on me like a mountain.

"Unknown or other" botulism is usually a case of adult intestinal toxemia. This variety is contracted the same way a baby gets infant botulism: the patient consumes food containing *C. botulinum* spores that find a favorable environment to germinate, most likely an unhealthy gut – such as a Crohn's patient's – as they do in the baby's immature intestines.

My former colorectal surgeon, Dr. Nguyen, who was on staff there and was looking in on my case, was the first to suggest that possibility. He told my wife, "I know George. He's not using heroin." He said he read some recent research into an unusually high incidence of "unknown and other" botulism cases in Crohn's patients. He theorized I hadn't fully recovered from Crohn's so was vulnerable and ingested some spores in something I ate.

The health authorities asked if there was honey in the house, which my wife turned over. I did have some of that honey the Friday before I fell ill, in some hot tea at lunch, but I thought the cause was something else. I also had some wine that evening that tasted bad and had some mold under the foil, and I wondered at the time if it might make me ill. Two weeks later, lying paralyzed in the ICU from whatever cause, my illness was infinitely worse than anything I feared that night.

Of course, there was no way to go back in time to follow me around and record everything I ate. And it didn't make any difference. We all understood there was no way to ever know for certain whether it was foodborne botulism, intestinal toxemia, or if I caught it from the environment, something in the wind.

While this drama played out around me, when I was awake I existed only in the moment. I did not experience the passage of time. It was always the present; things just happened to me. My mind had switched into a survival mode of trying to get through the current problem and enduring until I could be repositioned, have a lung treatment, get a pain shot, feel a warm hand on mine.

So, for a while, the days all seemed to be the same day. Doctors and nurses came and went; people took vital signs, changed IV bags. A rotating corps of respiratory techs visited several times a day to suction my airway clear and give me a breathing treatment. One of the regular RTs was the whistling guy, but I never heard his crazy little ditty again.

I was deathly afraid there would be another catastrophe and I would be alone and helpless when it did. I was monitored to prevent that, but being alone and paralyzed, surrounded by so many complicated systems necessary for keeping me alive, it always preyed on my mind that some small malfunction might shut down everything and kill me.

My family held the same fear and had already noticed problems. My daughter came in early one morning around five-thirty, and saw I wasn't lying in a normal posture. She discovered I was rolled over on top of my arm with the IV in it. Not only was I very uncomfortable, the needle had come out of the vein and the fluid formed a large bubble under my skin.

Then and there she decided that either she or her mother had to stay overnight with me until I stabilized, and for the remainder of my time in that facility one of them spent the entire night on a cot next to my bed. I remember one night, waking up and feeling relieved to realize my daughter was there, then listening to my little girl's soft breathing until I fell back asleep.

I knew nothing about the science of the *C. botulinum* spores and the way the toxin works. I first heard there was a "toxin" when Dr. Habibi mentioned the antitoxin. He said the antitoxin was coming in a few days from Los Angeles County Health Department where it was being produced, one dose, just for me. *It must be very powerful if it only takes one dose to fix this,* I thought.

The nurse came in to hang a new IV bag at an odd time that Sunday afternoon, and even though I was in a deep haze and she didn't say so, I knew she was setting up the infusion. I visualized the bag of clear fluid and the steady drip and the medicine running through the tube into my vein, thinking, *This is my ninth day in the hospital. I'm nine days into this and in nine days I'll be out* – it was actually the twelfth day, I lost three days in the turmoil – but I knew at the time I was just making a wish.

No one told me any such thing, and no one explained how the course of the disease would run or what comes next. No one told me I'd get better; I just presumed it. *They've given me the antitoxin. Isn't that the cure?* I expected to show signs of improvement very soon.

In the next day or so I noticed people were entering the room from a different direction and realized I had been moved to a new room. About the same time, an RT mentioned the tracheostomy in my neck – a long-term replacement for the ventilation tube inserted during my Code Blue – but I didn't know I had one. I was also surprised to learn they replaced the oral suction tube with a G-tube running directly into my stomach through the skin and abdominal wall. Due to the drug-induced haze, I was unaware I had undergone two significant surgeries. Now my gaping mouth was empty but could not close, while my eyes though filled with visions could not open.

While I waited for the antitoxin to raise me miraculously from this bed, my hopes were turning sour. I was still getting worse.

After the paralysis struck, I gave the doctor a weak thumbs-up the first night, although that ability was fading by the next day. Yet even after that, if my wife or daughter was holding my hand, they could feel me move my index finger a little. My wife developed a system of questions, which I would answer with one flex for "yes" or two for "no," to get essential information such as if I was in pain and where, was hot or cold, needed suction, or wanted to be turned. It was a lifeline of human contact to which I clung. Nevertheless, I could feel this limited response weaken further every day, even after I received the antitoxin.

That fragile connection with my family finally broke five days after the infusion. I expected to start regaining mobility, but instead the last faint embers went cold. I was completely immobile and unresponsive.

I had descended into a condition called Total Locked-In Syndrome. The classic locked-in patient is severely paralyzed, most often by a stroke, and can only communicate by moving their eyes or blinking. A few also retain some remnants of voluntary response in addition to their eyes. Being totally locked-in, I had no voluntary movement, no reflexes, I could not respond to any stimulus nor react to any danger, yet my consciousness was not affected. My body was shut down but brain activity was normal, and I remained aware of everything happening around me and to me.

Seeing me when I was totally locked-in, those young X-ray techs who left me toppled and twisted against the bed rail would perceive a patient indistinguishable from someone in a vegetative condition or minimally conscious state. In their eyes it would appear I possessed no awareness of what was happening to me or where I was and lacked the cognition even to physically sense the cold and pain they caused me.

I was devastated. I had been wondering what the timetable for recovery was but now it seemed there wasn't going to be a recovery. Nobody told me anything about progress or a prognosis, and I couldn't ask.

Being totally locked-in brought on a new terror: even surrounded by people, I could not feel more alone. I was a solitary prisoner, an exile from everyone I loved. I feared this was permanent and felt overwhelmed by a sense of futility and defeat.

One day, a hospital case manager came in and talked with my wife about plans for my transfer to a long-term acute care facility, or LTAC, and it dawned on me that the antitoxin just didn't do what I hoped. I was sure something went wrong.

With a sense of dread, I realized what the problem might be. Two or three days before my infusion, Dr. Nguyen suggested they flush out my intestines to clear out the bacteria and contaminated food still inside my paralyzed gut. But this wasn't done until six days after the infusion. I can't remember if anyone mentioned a reason for this delay, but I do recall that when Dr. Nguyen checked back on my case he was upset my medical team hadn't ordered it.

Therefore, to my mind it was possible there remained a lot of *C. botulinum* inside me – still producing fresh toxin – even after I got the antitoxin. I speculated that the additional toxin may have diluted the antitoxin below a therapeutic level or, because it entered my system after the infusion, undid its effect. If this was true it also meant, counting from the day I ingested the tea with honey and the bad tasting wine until the day of the intestinal flush, I had been saturated with the paralyzing poison for three weeks.

That was enough time for it to work its way into every fiber of my body and destroy every nerve connection susceptible to its effect. With that duration of exposure, I may have been dosed with more botulinum toxin than any person who ever had the disease and survived it.

As this whirlpool of disaster and isolation pulled me deeper into despair, I wondered if the course of the disease was complete and if being totally locked-in was going to be my future. A future in which I would exist, but in which I would not participate.

I was alone. It was afternoon; I knew it was a Sunday.

The door to my room was wide open, giving me a front row seat to a hospital reality show: they played the soundtrack out there, and I simply watched the movie in here, inside my head.

The background noises projected an imaginary map of the floor plan, and as the more distinct sounds came and went in the foreground, my mind's eye would follow the action across the screen. I visualized people's ages, clothing, and faces. I could picture the wall colors and spare equipment left in the corridors, the nurses' station and the different people working there. It was all as clear as if I were walking the halls. I didn't decide or consciously invent any of this; everything just appeared like a dream world, unbidden, lucid in every detail, a fully coherent unreality.

The same thing would happen when a nurse or tech was working in the room; a unique individual would spring to life from a name, a voice, a shadow. These visualizations were extraordinarily vivid in spite of my knowing they were imaginary. I wondered if I were hallucinating from the trauma or the drugs, and I often suspected that anything I "saw" in the room might have no connection to what was actually happening.

On that afternoon, the ongoing hospital drama was a distraction, but I wished they would come give me something to put me out for a while. I didn't want to think. I saw no prospect of positive change. In my mind I was still at the bottom of that hole.

Of the many different noises in the corridor, one set of approaching footsteps walked into the room. The visitor closed the door, shutting out the commotion, and silently stood toward my left. In the now-hushed room the only sound was a steady puff of air from the ventilator giving me my twenty breaths per minute. I had a premonition something had changed or was about to.

Because my right eye was slightly cracked open that day, I could see something of this apparition. It was in the far corner of my vision, and because I was not able to look directly at the visitor or focus my eye because of the paralysis, the image was very indistinct. I could tell this was someone new. It was a man, in white, probably wearing a lab coat. *Is he a doctor?* His complexion was dark and there was something white around his face; *Is it an isolation or surgical mask?* That he did not speak and did not move unsettled me, and the mask made him appear somewhat sinister.

The terror of being helpless in a life-and-death crisis was fresh and deep, and it seized my imagination. I thought, *Is this the angel of death come to finish his work, who will now disconnect me? Or someone who thinks he is the angel of death?*

My fear turned to confusion as he began to move his arms around, apparently purposefully. *Is he blessing me?* Maybe he was taking notes, but I couldn't see any paper or clipboard. I wondered if I was really seeing this. Then I thought, *Maybe he's not a doctor after all but an exorcist who heard about me and knows I'm actually cursed, who borrowed a doctor's jacket so he could sneak in here, and he's driving out the demon.* It was a silly thought of course, but at the same time I figured, *Go for it, brother. I need all the help I can get.* Within a few seconds his movements stopped.

Through the slit of my eye I saw him move across the room; I felt like the child who pretends to be sleeping when mom or dad peeks in. It occurred to me that maybe he really does think I am sleeping and is just being quiet, and he's not trying to scare me. As he passed in front of me I could make out he wore no mask; it had to be a white beard. He stopped on the right side of the bed, almost out of sight; I guessed he was looking down at me, and I think he again moved his arms in a deliberate way. *Is he praying?*

Then he stepped out of my field of vision farther back toward the ventilator. This was the one thing I needed to keep me alive, and I grew apprehensive again. Would I hear a click – the switch turning off – and then everything will go silent?

I felt a tension, an anticipation; something was about to happen. *What's going on? Who is he? Why is he here?*

I heard an intake of breath close to my ear.

"Hello, George. My name is Doctor Kumar. I will be taking care of you in the future." He paused. "You absolutely will get better."

With those last words I felt like a light went on inside me, like some dynamic force was flowing through every fiber of my being. I never felt anything like this before or since. This was a physical sensation yet at the same time something so emotionally or psychically affirmative it was startling. I immediately believed the doctor possessed or channeled a healing power, and he had just turned it on me, full blast. All at once I wanted to cheer, and I wanted to cry with gratitude. The warmth and joy I felt from my wife's gift of love several days earlier was only a preview of the energy bolt that struck me at that moment.

Believe me, this was not imaginary. I was infused with something very positive, maybe positivity itself, some fundamental life force. It struck me I was in the presence of a holy power, and I was receiving a second great gift – the first being love and now hope.

I didn't imagine what "better" meant beyond perhaps I'd breathe on my own, get out of this bed, see again. Someday. And the doctor just made that day a reality.

This was a marvelous thing: I was about to embark on the next traverse of my journey, long-term acute care, and here before the voyage begins was my new doctor telling me I absolutely will get across that foreign and perilous sea.

That Sunday afternoon I was drifting emotionally, passive in my mind, locked inside a body that looked more dead than alive, frightened, defeated, directionless. Then the doctor lit a beacon by which a lost soul might find his way home.

Part Three

Not long after Dr. Kumar left, the nurse told me I would be transferred to the long-term acute care facility the following day. It was the inevitable next step but still a grim prospect. Because, how long is long-term? One year? Two years?

In the evening my old surgeon, Dr. Nguyen, stopped in to see me, and say goodbye. I thought, *Wow, here it is Sunday night, and he is still seeing patients. And I'm not even his patient.*

"Hello, Mr. Walsh. I hear you're leaving us tomorrow," he said. His voice was professional and upbeat but with a definite tone of concern. "Well, Dr. Kumar is a good man. You're in good hands." Hearing this from someone I trusted was reassuring.

I felt his hand on my shoulder, and a gentle squeeze. "I know you're going through hell, my friend," he said, quietly. "Good luck, George. You're a great man."

"Great man"? I was stunned. That was the last thing I expected to hear. It didn't make sense. How would you react, if you were in my place? Me, the unemployed, totally locked-in loser. Why did he say it? My mind reeled.

Here was a man who saves lives, probably several times every week, who is brave enough to cut people open to ease their suffering, and he's calling me a "great man"?

I was embarrassed; it might be a joke, or he pities me. Then I thought, maybe he means I'm a great man generally speaking, like, I'm a good person. That, at least, was plausible. I did not reject his words. I felt flattered but didn't dwell on them or infer a deeper significance. For the time being it was amazing enough just to know – for some reason – this doctor believed in me.

The next evening the patient transport team arrived. I overheard some of their back-and-forth with the staff outside my door. There was a long delay for some paperwork. I was already nervous because my wife couldn't be there, and the extended wait made me more uneasy.

I wondered what the next place was like, if I would be warehoused with substandard care thanks to my insurance company. I worried the hospital might be far away and long drives would add to my family's burden.

My wait ended when into the room came the new voices along with some staffers' voices, and the sound of the gurney wheels and the rattle of its frame coming up next to me on the right, then I heard the snap and clatter of its railing being lowered. The bed buzzed until my head was down and I was stretched out flat. The move was underway.

The transport crew was two men and a woman; images of what they looked like sprang into my mind, their faces and physiques, their crisp white shirts with bold embroidered insignia. The woman introduced herself as the RT who would monitor my ventilator during the trip. It hadn't occurred to me, but of course I'd have to be on a respirator during the ride.

Then I felt and heard the thump of my bed rail going down.

"Ready?"

"Good."

"Get the board."

"Got it."

"Okay. To the patient's left."

I was rolled in that direction, and they slid something under me. I was rolled back onto a hard surface the length of my body. I had no padding on me, having lost sixty-five pounds from the Crohn's, and the edges of my shoulder blades and hips pressed painfully on the board. I could not move off the pressure points.

"Okay, let's get him up on the gurney. On three. One. Two. Three."

I felt myself smoothly lifted and swung sideways to my right, then tilted down on my side onto the gurney and the board sliding out. My back pain eased as I came down flat, sinking into the cushioned bed.

Several voices moved around me, and I felt hands and blankets pressing against me while I was rocked from side to side. I was being swaddled with sheets and blankets; they crossed my arms over my chest. Straps went snugly across them and over my legs, and I heard the *click-click* as the restraints were secured and a sharp crack close to my left ear when the gurney rail snapped into the upright position.

We began to move. I felt the sway and wobble of being up on a rolling gurney, the flowing sensation of its motion, its turning and maneuvering through the three-dimensional space I envisioned out there. I noticed the tingle of cool air on my face in the hallway, cooler still in the elevator, and when we came outdoors, the cold moist air of an early spring night.

The movement paused; I felt the wind brush the side of my face and heard its movement in the trees overhead, then noticed the sound of a vehicle nearby driving away, and even farther in the distance the insistent chaotic hum of roads and traffic – and I became terrified. As if I were alone and adrift on a limitless sea, I sensed the vastness of the world outside myself and its extreme danger to me in this condition. Thankfully the transport's doors opened, the gurney was pushed forward, and I felt the shake and heard the crash of the legs folding up under the bed as it slid into the ambulance. The doors boomed shut.

After a long ride cocooned in the transport listening to the crew's office gossip, I arrived at the new hospital. Two of the crew went inside while the driver came around and opened the doors. Feeling the outdoor air again and hearing the wind renewed my anxiety. I wanted to get inside the safe haven of a hospital room.

The driver stepped close behind me, and because I was up in the ambulance and he was standing down on the ground, his face was not far from mine when he spoke.

"I heard some good things about you back there, Mr. Walsh. You're a great man."

This echo of Dr. Nguyen's exact remark hit me like a slap. On the superficial level I wondered, *Who did he talk to? What did they say? They only know me through my family.* It made me happy to think the staff thought well of us.

On a deeper plane, I thought maybe he and the doctor just

wanted to encourage me, but it also seemed almost a taunt – those words reminded me how I once longed to be great and how keenly I felt my shortcomings. To mention me and "great man" in the same breath only emphasized the vast distance between that distinction and where I was now.

But then, from even farther down in my soul a thought arose that truly alarmed me: that this was a message from God telling me I had something to do beyond myself that I could not refuse. I don't think that's crazy; I believe even in your normal, everyday life, you too would consider it more than a coincidence if two different, unconnected people said the exact same, extremely meaningful thing to you in the course of a single day. Now, think of what it meant to someone in my circumstances. Being in such desperate straits I was searching for cosmic meaning, signs from above, some explanation for why this happened. I recognized this in myself, so I was skeptical I was some chosen person while at the same time worried it may be true.

I wanted to evade this obligation I felt pressing in on me. *Can't you just leave me here in my misery? Don't you see I have nothing to give?*

Like an immune reaction fighting off a virus, my mind mobilized different ways to explain it away. *It's only a coincidence they used the same words. They just feel sorry for me. It's the nicest thing they could think to say.* But then I hit on an idea that made me feel free: *I'm great because I am suffering. Yes, that's it – I'm like a saint!*

It was a flattering and seductive thought. It answered all my worries at once: If I am great now, I am also automatically, instantly absolved of my past failures and relieved of any responsibilities for the future. I need do nothing further, not even think about it. This was intoxicating – it filled me with a warm glow of smug self-satisfaction more soothing than a pain shot.

The feeling lasted but a split second. I suddenly felt an excruciating sensation as if I were under microscopic scrutiny or caught in a searchlight with nowhere to hide. It was like being called out by a teammate to get my head in the game, a rival telling me to put up or shut up. I was embarrassed by my magical thinking, for pretending victimhood bestows virtue. I was confronted with the sobering reality of all the work and time looming in front of me until I can go home again – if I get home again.

I realized being great isn't a compliment.

It's a mountain to climb.

With a jolt the gurney began moving again, and the legs snapped loudly into place. It startled me, bringing me back into the moment. A few bumpy feet farther and we passed through the two sets of automatic doors. I heard the swoosh of their opening, and felt the warm indoor air and the rumbles of the wheels across the thresholds as I came into this place that was going to be my home for who knows how long.

I don't know what Dr. Nguyen and the transport driver intended when they called me a "great man," but I do know the result. My thinking shifted. The effect wasn't like a light going on or a burst of energy, but more of a sea change in my mind. The course of an underlying current had turned.

Their words reminded me there were some things in the past I did do right. Job one was being a good dad to my kids and a faithful family man, and I gave it my all; I was a long-time volunteer youth soccer referee, senior instructor and board member; I even hit a few home runs back in the business world, back in the day. In the midst of this chaos and pain it was sweet to experience a little bit of pride again. By making me feel better about myself, they saved me from the debilitating poison of self-pity.

They also put a frame around my situation, giving me a new perspective. Just by mentioning me and greatness in the same breath, they gave me a standard to measure myself going forward – regardless of how I do. In this way, although I thought they were talking about my past, they made me think ahead. I gained the clarity to begin preparing myself for the challenge I faced.

I accepted that I had lost everything physically, for now, but looked for what I could gain, both physically and spiritually. *Will I walk again? Will I be a better person?*

I realized there was one thing I still had the capability to do: I could choose my attitude. Because my spirit had been buoyed by three great gifts – love, hope, and now purpose – my mind turned toward the positive.

I steeled myself for a long hospital stay. I knew that as these interminable days slowly pass, I must forgive errors and misunderstandings, endure pain and isolation. Through the coming frustration and all the waiting, I must be patient; through the indignities of helplessness, grateful for life and for others' compassion. Above all, I must not despair.

It was difficult being positive, there in my new home, again in an ICU. My life was on a delicate balance and my care regimen extremely complex. Any upset to the equilibrium – caused either by my body's weaknesses, equipment malfunction, or a caregiver's mistake or negligence – might precipitate a cascade of system failures that could result in my death.

The top issue was my breathing. Actually, I didn't breathe; I was ventilated. My chest went up and down about twenty times per minute exchanging oxygen and carbon dioxide. This was the main reason I was here; it was imperative the respirator keep running.

I was joined to the respirator through a tracheostomy at the base of my neck, and the dressing and the area around the tube needed to be regularly sterilized. The various air tubes and connectors did not snap or fasten but only slipped together, and since their insides got wet from the ventilator's humidified air, those connections were subject to slipping apart. Such an event could sever my air flow and my life.

My lungs were always congested, which limited my capacity and made me almost always feel I was suffocating. Temporary relief came every six hours when a respiratory therapist suctioned out my lungs. This chronic congestion made me more vulnerable to pneumonia, always a danger in a long hospital stay but especially so in this place full of very sick people.

Dr. Kumar was also concerned about a pocket of excess fluid inside my chest, called a pleural effusion, which limited my lung capacity even further. Suction had no effect on this problem. It was worse on the right, and that lung had much less volume than the left.

To minimize the chest fluid, the doctor set the IV at a very slow drip. This kept me borderline dehydrated, and my mouth – which was always open – was terribly dry all the time. The underlying cause of this desperate thirst was the botulism itself; it had turned off my salivary glands. The weakened, commercial version of the toxin, Botox, is sometimes used to control excessive salivating caused by certain conditions, and I got extended exposure to the pure-strength formula.

My intestines were paralyzed but they still produced digestive juices. Without a way to remove these fluids, at minimum the build-up caused painful bloating. Worse, they would eventually rise up in the esophagus and spill over into my trachea and lungs. The certain result is aspiration pneumonia, a particularly bad form, and the acidic fluids would also damage the delicate trachea and bronchi.

To prevent that, I had a G-tube running directly through the abdominal wall into my stomach, connected to a suction pump. I already had two long scars forming a cross over my belly from my three major surgeries (one incision was repurposed by Dr. Miles), as well as two shorter horizontal ostomy scars on the upper left. Together they looked like a letter from an ancient alphabet carved into my body. This new hole was a mere punctuation mark, but it created another infection risk.

The G-tube had a side port through which most of my twenty-six daily medications and supplements were administered. Twice each day the LVN crushed the pills in a cup, added water, poured it into a large syringe, and injected it into me. But to allow me to absorb the meds they first needed to turn off the suction pump; otherwise the medicines would be sucked away immediately. Then they needed to come back in about an hour to turn it back on before I started to bloat and the countdown to aspirating stomach acid began. Sometimes they forgot to come back on time, and if no family was with me, I could only hope somebody returned before it was too late.

Adding to this complexity, the pump frequently developed an air leak along the tubing or connectors that broke the vacuum seal and stopped the sucking, while still making noises like everything was working just fine. To confirm fluid was coming out of me, the nurse had to walk over and examine the pump, rather than just glance over and listen for the noise – if they even knew there was such a problem to check in the first place.

My intestines could absorb medicine but not enough

nutrition to keep me alive. I was nourished with TPN through a picc line, just as I was during the later stages of my battle with Crohn's. Having an IV line running deep into my chest was a constant risk of serious infection. A picc line is like a germ highway straight to your heart.

Although I could subsist on TPN, it would not provide enough sustenance to maintain my already unhealthy low weight. My Crohn's-battered body was getting weaker by the day, setting back the starting point of any potential recovery.

Pain shots and certain other medications were delivered through an IV line that was always running saline solution. The IV site had to be changed every three to five days; the insertions hurt but were tolerable. Though well protected, the active site was another infection risk. The continual changing of sites from the left arm to the right and back, over and over – plus blood draws for lab work every few days – caused the veins to collapse. Over time, this made it increasingly difficult to find a vein, which was already a problem since I was so underweight.

I was taking in fluids and my kidneys worked but I could not urinate. My muscles were clamped shut. The best solution for my long-term situation was to insert a Foley catheter into my bladder. Urinary tract infections are very easy to develop with catheters, so they need to be changed every several weeks, which was the least favorite part of having one. There was also an issue arising from my needing one far longer than normal: whether I can regain bladder control if the muscles are only weakened before it's removed – or not, if the muscles become atrophied by then. It was possible I could never do it again without some aid, or it will never stop and I'd have to live with that embarrassment.

I had been weaned off the most powerful pain drugs like propofol and now could feel a deep ache throughout my body. This continual and comprehensive pain was exhausting, which was probably why I slept so much. My entire skeleton hurt; my joints were very painful whenever I was moved and my range of motion was severely limited. The worst pain was in my lower back and hips, and in my shoulders and neck.

Every part of me felt clenched. My hands were distorted into fists, curled down at the wrist. My tongue was contracted all the way to the back of my mouth. My head was thrown back and my mouth gaped open – both were still in the same positions they were put in for my intubation, locked in place during those critical minutes by the rapid onset of paralysis.

For pain I was given two principal medications, fentanyl, an opioid transdermal patch for relief around the clock, and IV injections every two hours on the hour of Dilaudid, which is made from morphine.

These helped me tolerate the pain, get what rest I could and, frankly, pass the time. Both are narcotics, which slow respiration as well as intestinal activity, also called gastric motility. This effect was not an issue while I was still paralyzed, but someday I might face a trade-off: I may need to quit the narcotics and deal with pain to help my diaphragm and intestines start functioning again.

All these many issues were just the ones we knew of and problems we hoped to prevent, but the worst thing to happen to me in the ICU was unexpected, even random. I was being well and kindly cared for when the accident occurred, during one of the few moments of precious comfort I enjoyed each day.

I was getting a sponge bath. That evening some of the bed sheets were bunched up close to my head on my right. Too close. This was of no consequence until the nurse turned me onto that side. As I turned, to my horror a vertical fold of the jumbled sheet got caught underneath my partially-open eyelid, sliding it fully open – and I felt the shocking friction of my exposed eyeball getting dragged across the rough fabric.

The pain was sudden and sharp – and I could not flinch, or close the eye, or cry out despite the agony. Piercing deeply into my brain was the terror that I would be blinded or disfigured. Tears flooded from the wounded eye, and I wished I could move away even a millimeter or just blink. The pain pulsed sharply while my vision was filled with an extreme close-up of the sheet's woven fibers in a color gradient of ivory to white.

The bath continued, the nurse unaware of what happened. Soon I was laid back flat; the eyelid flopped down, hiding the wound. I got a pain shot, and the lights went out.

At the last hospital, in my imposed darkness I imagined in extreme detail what the facility looked like. As you'd expect, it was a normal healthcare environment including a busy nurses' station, hallways scattered with spare IV poles and vitals monitors recharging, my room's stark walls of gray and beige, colorless vinyl flooring, ceilings panels glaring with harsh fluorescent lights.

Here, in my mind's eye, my new room had beautiful hardwood flooring in a warm light oak color. To my right was a large window with floor-length curtains next to tall shelves stocked with books of various sizes and different colors. Along the right side of the bed, an elegant swiveling armchair in black leather was complemented by a glass coffee table, a stylish and modern design. The room's soaring, sloped ceiling featured large exposed wooden beams that extended into the spacious, well-lit open-plan office outside the room. There were half-wall dividers between the work stations, capped with leafy plants. On the far side of that space was a bright wall of windows looking onto a parking lot. The wall of my room on the corridor side was also all glass, including the door. It didn't look at all like a real hospital, but more of a suburban branch bank with an atrium or skylight in the center, and I was in one of the peripheral offices.

Of course, none of that was true. Yet, it did not seem strange or surprising to me at the time. I must have mistakenly decided "long-term acute care" was not carried out at a regular hospital, freeing my mind to visualize something different. Then, whatever scraps of visual information I could gather, distorted by the pain medications, sent my imagination opposite from reality. What else would explain my belief there was a parking lot out there, when we were on the third floor?

Oddly, it wasn't in my drugged dreams but in more lucid moments when I "saw" the strangest thing of all – something going on right in front of me that, while it was happening, I knew was impossible.

I've mentioned that sometimes I could detect movement and see vague fragments of color, light, and shadow through the tiny slit of a cracked-open right eyelid. During the daytime, when the only light was coming in sideways from the window, someone walking across my arc of vision appeared as a pair of blurs, one bright and one dark, corresponding to the illuminated side of the figure and the shadow side. In addition, my damaged eye produced teardrops, which collected at the base of my lashes; these small round drops formed a lens that flipped the images like a magnifying glass or microscope does.

Now, this only happened over just two or three days and only two or three times, but if someone came in when all the conditions were perfect – the opening of the slit, the size of the teardrops, the angle of daylight – when that pair of light and dark blurs moved briskly past me, I saw my two dogs running by.

Both dogs are about the same size, miniature Schnauzers,

mostly, and one is white and one is dark gray. Light and shadow, white and gray, a mis-matched pair . . . at the time it must have made sense somewhere in my brain. As if that was normal – when I happen to be paralyzed and lying in a hospital and can only see a sliver of light, any bright and dark shapes passing through my room obviously have to be my dogs, right?

Making it even crazier, don't forget the teardrops refracted the light, inverting the image – so there were my pups, running by, upside down across the ceiling.

It was a nice surprise to be reminded of them, although a sad one since it made me miss them. But what a strange way to be reminded!

Imagine walking into my room in the ICU; you see me lying there. Close the door, hush the hospital noise, and the loudest sound you hear is the breathing of the ventilator. The body you look upon is stiff, looking quite like a corpse except for such signs as the pinkish tone in the gray skin, the chest rising at a steady rate, the drip of the IV, and a blinking number on the pulse monitor.

You know I am alive but you might assume – it is so easy to assume – that the body before you is oblivious, in a coma perhaps, as insensate as it is immobile. You may believe I inhabit a different world than yours and am not aware you are there with me.

As you look down at me, now also imagine you are responsible for my health regime for the next twelve hours, the intake of nutrition, medicines, and air, and including the physical maintenance of my body. Add to this the fact that I am just one of your patients on your shift, all in much the same condition as this poor soul. Even though you chose this profession to care for others and feel the deepest compassion for all of them, it is necessary to turn down the level of emotional involvement. To armor yourself against the stress and sadness, you must block out feelings about the patient as an individual – the three-dimensional, once-walking, formerly talking, unique personality whom this patient truly is.

I expect this is a common reaction, and normal. We all understand this. Indeed, each patient has a tragic story yet each looks to the caregiver to be strong. This is even truer in transitional care because so many patients must stay for a long time and many will not get much better.

In such a job where it is easy to become desensitized, anything that will remind the individual on staff that a patient is a real person and make them engage on a personal level must be beneficial for the patient. This is not to say the nurse or therapist will care more. Rather, the patient will get more care.

My wife and I had noticed this the previous February when I was admitted with Crohn's, and we met the surgeon they called in to consult in case the abscess needed surgery. My wife introduced herself and reminded him they had met; she did his wife's OB ultrasounds a few years earlier. He remembered and began using her first name. I thought, *Well, he's going to take a special interest now. I'm more than a case; I'm practically family.*

In my current situation, ever since I had been rolled onto my IV arm at the previous hospital, my family was concerned the opposite would occur. They thought if someone thought I was totally out of it, and therefore could not give any feedback if I were mistreated, there was a greater chance they'd be careless or neglectful. To promote more attentive care, they needed to somehow inform the staff that this living mannequin on their hands was not only still human but wholly cognizant of their actions as well.

My daughter found a way to speak for me, humanize me, and

address the awareness issue. The idea came from a conversation with a nurse at the first hospital who suggested we put a sign above me saying, "Hi, I'm alert and can hear everything, so please tell me who you are and why you are here."

My daughter expanded that idea and created on her computer a poster to hang above the bedside table. It pretended to be a message from me, beginning with me introducing myself. It mentioned some key details of my life: father of twins; worked in marketing as an executive, writer, and graphic artist; refereed soccer; plays piano and guitar. It included a photo of me and my little grandson showing me playing guitar and him a ukulele. We both wear dark-framed glasses so there is a noticeable resemblance even from a casual glance.

In bold type it stated I am paralyzed but not brain-damaged, I can hear, and I'm aware of everything going on in the room.

It was heartening to me when a nurse or assistant or therapist read this. I would hear an appreciative tone if they read it aloud, or a chuckle after they finished reading, as if they were thinking, "Well, what do you know? That's new; how interesting to put up a poster like this. So that's who this guy is."

Now, before them wasn't just another patient. Here was an entire life. It made me proud of my daughter when they then turned toward me and said, with a friendly tone like in a normal conversation, "Well, I'm glad to meet you, Mr. Walsh."

My nephew came to visit me on one of my first days in the new ICU. He sat down in the stylish imaginary black leather armchair and talked a little. I don't recall what he said. I was just happy he stopped in, yet, for the first time, I was embarrassed to be seen like this.

He's the same age as our twins; they all grew up together and are still close. He and his mom were at our place all the time when he was young for barbecues, birthday parties, and sleepovers. He'd join us on many camping trips too, when we'd hike, eat a lot, sing songs, tell stories, and gaze up at the stars.

My nephew has a tragic circumstance in his life. Before his second birthday, his father, my brother-in-law, was hit by another vehicle while riding his motorcycle and suffered a major head injury. The boy was deprived of the engaged dad he would have had, whom every child deserves. Thanks to his remarkable mother, he has grown into an admirable, hardworking, and level-headed young man.

After a while, the RN came in. She introduced herself and he told her his name.

"Well it's good to meet you," she said. Then she asked, "Are you his son?"

"No, I'm his nephew," he replied. "But in many ways, he has

been like a father to me."

I wanted to jump off the bed and hug that kid. It broke my heart that I couldn't even look at him. Considering the type of man he had become, this was one of the nicest things anyone ever said to me. I was honored and grateful, and my pride in him grew.

Then I was caught in an emotional riptide. The drama of finding, at this specific moment in time, by just being myself I had that important and positive influence on him, was almost unbelievable. I thought, *How can I experience such a fantastic thing at the lowest point in my life?* It seemed impossible this happiness could exist amid the horror of my illness, but I wouldn't have learned this if I hadn't gotten so sick. The horror had brought forth the happiness.

My mind reeled at the mystery of it, and from the impact of experiencing such a range of conflicting emotions in a single instant.

Dr. Kumar said I "absolutely will get better," and his conviction became a beacon to guide me through this dangerous passage. Although it guides you to shore, however, a beacon does not illuminate what your life will be like when you land. Nor does it show you how to make your crossing.

It was my first morning at the new hospital when I met Doctor Barone, the man in charge of my rehab program. I could not see him, only his gesturing hand, a shadow circling against the brightness of the window. I was in a very hazy state and didn't know who he was or what he was saying, but I sensed this talkative visitor was important.

I learned nothing from him that day about my condition or his plan. Instead, my first understanding of how rehab is supposed to help me came from my occupational therapist.

"Hi, Mr. Walsh. Good morning. My name is Laurie. I'm going to be your primary occupational therapist while you are with us," she said. She was energetic and upbeat. "There are more of us, but mostly it will be me for your OT. We'll work on your arms and hands, while the PTs, the physical therapists, work on your lower body."

The disembodied voice floating above me on my left was professional, practiced. She projected confidence. I imagined she was mid-thirties, and from her spirited manner of speaking, and her being a therapist, I guessed she was into fitness or athletics.

"I don't know how much detail Dr. Barone told you about the therapy part of this, so I'll explain what's going to happen and what we're trying to do," she said. She slid her hands under my elbow and upper arm. "While I explain, I'm also going to work with you a bit and check your flexibility. I want to see what we're dealing with." She lifted the arm slightly. I felt a sharp jolt of pain in my shoulder joint. "Oh, yeah. That's tight. That's going to need some extra attention," she said with enthusiasm. She gently repeated the movement as she continued her lesson.

"Apart from the disease that paralyzed you, just being motionless damages the body. The joints could freeze up permanently, and the muscles atrophy past the point of being able to regenerate." This news frightened me, and I tried to listen more closely. "Your physical therapists and I will come in several times a week to move your body around, to keep you flexible and increase your range of motion. Like on this shoulder.

"The other benefit is that by moving the body, it stimulates the nerves to reconnect with the muscles. The nerves grow new connections."

She said this with no emphasis, but my mind latched on to every word. *Did she just say what I think she said? Is this the process how I get better, as Dr. Kumar promised?*

"That's just the start of the program, of course. The goal is to get you moving on your own again, right?" I pictured her shrugging. She took my hand and began to carefully straighten it out and then curl it into a fist. I felt stinging bolts of pain from the fingertips back to my wrist. "After the first new connections are made, and you're able to move a little under your own power, we combine therapy with exercise and you take over more of the work." Her voice became more earnest. "The more you exercise, the more connections you'll regrow, and the faster you do it the more you'll reconnect."

She seemed excited now, excited for me, challenging me and encouraging me at the same time. "That means your own personal effort will be the biggest factor in determining how far you come back, and how much mobility and independence you regain."

She came around the bed and worked on my other arm and hand, blocking the brightness of the window. Her monologue shifted to the specifics of the treatment. I tried to ignore the pain and considered what she said.

I knew the botulinum toxin had shut down the nerves, but not how the process worked. In my mind I saw a nerve cell with its long tendrils lifeless and withered. Now I visualized new branches growing, reaching out to touch the muscle. It made sense. This was vital, fundamental information about my disease that offered hope for a very positive outcome. I understood but didn't get emotional. Or couldn't. What clicked in my mind was the practical aspect of it. I knew I could get to work right away.

When Laurie said I must use any capability of my own to make myself better, I had a revelation. I realized I could move my eyes. I remembered I had followed a bit of Dr. Kumar's movement past the foot of my bed a few days earlier, and had tried to look toward Laurie when she came in. Therefore, I already could do something to help myself. I could start exercising my eye muscles until they're strong enough to work normally, to resolve my double vision.

I began as soon as she left. No one knew it except me, but many times each day and even at night I was "working out" inside my eyelids. I did repeated sets, moving my eyes as far as they could go, up and down or left to right, or circles in each direction, even triangles. I knew it was going to be a while until my eyes reopened and my hypothesis could be tested, but an immediate positive benefit was my mind became engaged in my own care. Besides the physical benefits, having work to do helped push away the shadows of fear and depression that were still and at all times pressing in on me.

This activity was the first thing I could do for myself since texting that nurse I was having trouble breathing.

A week to ten days later, I could feel movement in my tongue again. Applying my new knowledge, I concentrated on stretching it out, over and over, trying to go farther every time. My objective was to straighten it enough to touch my bottom teeth. It had to be little more than an inch but seemed so far.

I thought it was funny how no one knew what I was doing, but inside this static shell I was working hard. The effort paid off when just a few days later the tongue reached the gum, and the next day when I once again felt the familiar ridged texture of the back of my bottom teeth.

I should have been happy, even excited – this was the first

goal I set and achieved in my fight to overcome paralysis. But I was very tired and my mind was drifting away, I was numbed by pain killers and antidepressives, so felt nothing, and thought almost nothing about this accomplishment except that it was done.

Other than the fear of dying, among the most emotionally upsetting aspects of my paralysis was my isolation. I was surrounded by people but separated from them by an invisible wall. This solitude was one of the most bitter aspects of being totally locked-in.

In that state, I was in the world but not of it. I existed inside a shell lying in a dark void that had no boundaries – yet I was there in the room, in the present, experiencing my helplessness, aware of what was happening and those around me. The possibility that I might be forever cut off from other people in this way was a real-life version of a horror story from my childhood: the tale of a man being buried alive because they believe he's dead, and they don't notice his eyes moving through the little window in the coffin when they lower him down.

It was eerie to have people talking around me and over me about me, discussing grave issues about my life and health, making critical decisions about my future without my input. Sometimes they'd talk directly to me, explaining what is wrong, what they're going to do – while inside my wildly spinning brain I'm answering them, expressing opinions, asking questions. It was frustrating and frightening to be only a spectator to your own full-on long-term life-support medical crisis.

Then, one day perhaps two weeks after my tongue began to reactivate, I was visualizing my hand and how I used to make it move. I tried to get the part of my index finger near the base to tighten, to curl in, and on one attempt it did feel like it moved. It was so slight I thought I might be imagining it. I tried it again and this time I was sure.

I started exercising it like I was my eyes and tongue, only with more purpose, because a hand signal would have more immediate benefits. If I could make it move far enough for others to see or feel, I'd be able to give feedback to improve my comfort and care. Just as important, I'd have a connection with other people and ease the worst of my loneliness.

I knew it would be my little secret until the right opportunity, when the movement was strong enough and someone was holding my hand. Several days later I had that chance, when my wife came in and, as she greeted me, took my right hand and gave it a squeeze.

"Hi, sweetie. Good morning." I felt her free hand wipe the sweat from my forehead. "I hope they treated you well during the night." I quickly tried to flex my index finger in response, thinking that at this moment, she'd realize it wasn't a random movement – if she noticed it.

I felt her hand in mine freeze up, like she was trying to hear a whisper with her fingers. "Geo? Did they treat you well last night?" she asked again. I made one flex. "Oh! Geo, you can move your hand again?" One flex. She laughed with surprise and relief. "Or a finger. Oh, wow! Oh, Geo, this is great!"

Her jubilant tone turned serious. She quickly asked, "Are

you cold?" I flexed my finger to answer her. "Are you hot? Are you in pain? Is it in your upper body?" Without skipping a beat, she started using her system of yes-no questions as if she had been expecting this all along. Having to concentrate on her questions and make my responses clear, I didn't have time to feel happy for this breakthrough.

With more therapy and exercise, soon the faint flexing strengthened until I could make the knuckles of both my index and middle fingers rise up in a quick and definite motion. It may have been no more than a centimeter, but anyone could see it. When my wife saw I could signal to the staff, she wrote up her list of questions and posted it on the wall next to my bed, alongside my daughter's poster. Anyone on staff could follow her system to determine my needs. They asked, and I answered with one twitch for "yes" or two for "no."

I was no longer buried alive. After two months of being totally locked-in, I could finally answer back from the bottom of this hole to the people calling down to me.

The flood waters having begun to ebb, I was moved down the hall into a new room. I was no longer in ICU but on the same floor and still monitored.

I don't remember being moved, just waking up in a new room during the night, awakened by the screams of a woman somewhere nearby. I think it happened several times the same night and the following night as well. She seemed to be in the next room behind my head, just a few feet away, screaming in agony or from dementia or God knows why.

My experience continued to be one of long stretches of unconsciousness or semi-awareness pierced by occasional phases of intense mindfulness. From the depths of a troubled sleep I would awaken into fragmented moments of discomfort or pain; of unseen hands on my body moving me, turning me over; of another needle going in my arm; of the sounds of routine events occurring around me over and over and quickly forgotten. I was always hurting and short of breath, always waiting for someone to show up and ask the right question to fix some problem I could not explain.

The overall passage of time was not a part of my thinking because each day was itself an exhausting obstacle course. Or maybe more like river rafting through white water: I'm hurtling toward dangers that buffet and batter me, while I'm unable to stop and there's no way out.

The ICU was an oasis of calm compared to the general section. In this part of the hospital there was much more commotion in the hallway. Carts, staff, and visitors were continually passing by. People were frequently talking loudly and calling out. The PA system blared almost constantly and there was even a speaker in the room. The mad, insistent beeping of a stalled IV pump somewhere on the floor was a regular occurrence. I was near some closets or cabinets that were always being used including slamming the door. And I was in the very heart of this cyclone because my room was across the hall from the nurses' station, the communication center and hub of all activity.

I was not buffered from the noise in the least because for easy access they always left my door open, whereas in ICU the doors were always closed. There was also a large window on the corridor-side wall, further exposing me. It was like being in a fishbowl next to the busiest place in the hospital, a rare medical specimen on display.

My daily routine was a repetitious but juggled agenda. Dr. Kumar came in almost every day; Dr. Barone about twice a week. Nurses changed IV bags and gave me pain shots; the LVNs crushed my pills and injected them into my G-tube; people turned the suction pump off and on. CNAs cleaned me, rolled me back and forth to change the sheets, and took vitals every four hours. Someone propped me up on one side with foam wedges for a while, then turned me the other way; it was uncomfortable to be on my side, but they said it helped keep my lungs clearer. An RT came in twice each shift for a breathing treatment and suction. My occupational and physical therapists each saw me several times every week. Other people came to take out the trash, someone else to mop the floor. Every morning a person stocked my medicine cabinet. Every few days around four in the morning a tech came in to draw blood for lab work, a cheerful vampire.

Within this controlled chaos it was very hard to rest, even in the relative quiet of night. My body craved sleep but I could not rest more than two hours in a row, day or night.

Nevertheless, this room did offer a vital advantage: it was for a single patient, while most of the rooms here were doubles. I was in such a daze I didn't realize how important that was for someone in my condition, but my wife did. That's why, when she showed up unexpectedly one night at around nine o'clock, she was shocked to catch them in the process of moving me. They had already rolled my bed, with me in it, into the hall when she arrived.

I was not aware they were moving me, but noticing my wife was there and that she was upset roused me from my drugged stupor. I heard her voice above and behind me, and its undercurrents of anger and will power. "No, you are not moving him. No. No way. I refuse," she was insisting. "We have the right to refuse and his condition is too fragile, so I refuse. Put him back. Put him back."

There were replies from far away I could not understand. Now my wife sounded indignant as she hammered home her reasoning. "He's on a respirator, G-tube, IV, Foley, he's paralyzed – there is no way you can put him in a double. That increases his risk of infection, being exposed to another sick patient plus his visitors and the additional staff coming and going. And for who knows how long? No, that's too dangerous. It's crazy! He's staying here."

She stopped the move that time, but we knew since I was a high-maintenance patient on an expensive ventilator who would be here a long time, hospital management would try to push me to a less-costly room as soon as they could.

She was determined to prevent it. I remember her telling me, perhaps the next day, because the room was quite bright then, "They'll probably try it again, to sneak you to a new room in the middle of the night without telling me. Just like they did when they put you here. But I'm not going to let them move you, honey. I'm not going to let them."

My condition seemed relatively stable now, and my wife and daughter thought it was safe to spend less time at the hospital. They even skipped some days. But a few bad incidents in my early weeks in the new room compelled them to renew their vigilance and become more closely involved in supervising my day-to-day routine.

In the first episode my wife arrived in the late afternoon to discover an ugly stain soaking the gown and beddings, and found I was lying in a pool of gastric juices from a leaking or malfunctioning G-tube. The acidic fluid was harsh on the skin; I felt a sharp irritation at the entry site but had no idea what was happening. When my wife found this and realized it had been going on for several hours and obviously nobody checked on me during that time, she blew her top.

"I can't believe this! I *can't* believe this!" Her hand landed on the rail, rattling the entire bed. "I can *not* believe this!" she fumed as she moved quickly toward the door. The swirl of hospital noises flooded in when it opened.

Her voice rang out over the clamor of the hallway and nurses' station. "Who is his nurse? Who is *his nurse!*" There was a pause. "Because I need to see his nurse immediately! Who's the charge nurse? I want to see the charge nurse too!" I heard concerned voices approaching, coming into the room, then my wife's voice suddenly close to the bed. "There, he's lying in gastric juices! Look at this, he's lying in a pool of stomach acid. And for how long? This had to be *hours!* I want him cleaned up and these sheets changed stat!"

There were some apologetic noises from the staffers, then her voice turned colder and she spoke slowly. "I am *not* going to tolerate this *neglect*. If anything like this happens again you are not to work with him, you are not to *touch* him, again!"

A voice next to the bed said, "Yes, Mrs. Walsh. I'll get the CNA," and moved away. An older voice remained, making assurances.

I remember the second event more clearly; you might say it made an impression.

At the time I didn't know this, but at the first hospital I had developed a bedsore at the bottom of my spine. I was in pain everywhere so didn't notice. On the day of this second event, the pulse oximeter sensor was clipped to a toe on my right foot while the display monitor was on the nightstand at the head of the bed on the left. To cover this distance required two cables joined by a connector, a cube about two inches on each side with square edges.

It began when the nurse or attendant turned me onto my right side for some reason. This movement dragged the cable across the middle of the bed; no one noticed. When I was laid flat again, the cable was still under me with the connector box directly below the bedsore – and as I came down on it, it felt like a hot knife going into my back. It is so strange to feel intense pain while it is inflicted and have to passively accept it, to be unable to jump up screaming, to experience the agony in its fullness and as it goes on interminably. I did not know about the bedsore, so I had no idea what happened and why I was in such pain. I felt panicky.

My head was spinning for I don't know how long until my wife came in. She immediately knew I was in great distress. I could not answer her usual questions, so she did an inspection. Eventually she rolled me on my side and discovered the connector laying under me, its square outline cut into the raw and seeping wound.

"Oh, no. Oh, no!" she gasped. Now that I was on my side and the pain had suddenly stopped, I was ready to pass out in relief. In a moment, I heard the *shick, shick* sound her phone made when taking a picture. She was getting photographic documentation of the injury.

By her breathing I heard her turn away. "Damn them!" she exclaimed in anger, and I heard something large clatter across the floor and bang against the wall, a chair, I guessed. The door opened and the rush of hospital sounds engulfed me. The sharp, manic alarm of an IV pump somewhere down the hall underscored the stress in the air. My wife began calling from the door to get someone's attention, but there was a difference from the gastric juices incident. Her voice was raised but the volume and outrage were less, replaced by an urgent and authoritative tone. It sounded as if now, after these repeated problems, her anger had been tempered into a hard resolve. I caught a few clipped words: "Yes .

.. serious problem . . . injury."

Soon the room was filled with many voices. My wife was repeatedly asking, "Who did this? Who did this?" I recall a high-level supervisor came in, and my wife dictating her terms, "I want the change now, and I don't want any of them coming near my husband again." She must have demanded they change my nursing crew that day and never assign those individuals to me going forward. From the supervisor's tone, it seemed they would do just as she wished.

But speaking up would not be enough to protect me. My issues were complex even for the regular staff, but this hospital chain also used a large number of per diem and registry nurses. They came in knowing nothing about my condition and the complexities of my care, such as the gastric pump timing and its air leaks. With workers drawn from such a deep pool, the quality of care I received on any given day ranged from excellent to substandard.

In light of this inconsistent care, and after these two incidents and the hospital trying to secretly move me, my wife and daughter made a big decision. For my safety and to ensure continuity and accountability, they decided that one or the other must be at the hospital every day for each change of shift – which is two round trips each day – to brief my nurse for that shift on all the specific complications they needed to watch for and manage. Their presence would also make it harder for management to sneak me to a double room.

From that day forward, one of them would always be at

my bedside by seven o'clock, both a.m. and p.m., with only rare exceptions. They worked as one to supervise my care and kept each other appraised of changes in my condition and of notable events or emergent issues, so were both up to speed whenever either came in. On most days, one was there when Dr. Kumar made his rounds, so both were intimately aware of the big picture as well as the details of my status and treatments.

On many of my daughter's days, she would appear at five or six in the morning. That is sort of a surprise inspection; no one expects you then. She kept the list of staff incidents and of people whom they blackballed from ever working with me again. She also had power of attorney so she could approve a particular procedure or treatment for me when a timely decision was needed.

My daughter was a real networker; she visited with the staff at the nurses' station or in the hall, or chatted them up when they came in, getting to know the reputations of who is good at their job and who isn't. She specialized in gathering behind-the-scenes information on hospital goings-on that might be useful. She learned about the professional staff's labor organizing effort and made a lot of new best friends when she showed up at their pro-union demonstration. She can turn on her professional-level charm to win people over, but she also knows how to smile sweetly while icily telling someone they're doing something wrong and they better freaking fix it. Right. Now.

My wife juggled patients and extended her week so she could be at the hospital twice each day on her days, which was at least five days each week. In contrast with my daughter's style when problems occurred, my wife got demonstrably angry when something went wrong on her watch. The issues that ticked her off ranged from actual incompetence, of which there was an unfortunately ample supply, to a disrespectful or indifferent attitude, which was so hurtful. Although there were times I thought she went on too long and I got embarrassed, those feelings were eclipsed by the reassurance I received and my gratitude. Knowing that this woman was fighting to defend my life filled me with deep humility and awesome pride.

As they coordinated their daily visits and updated each other, my wife and daughter came to form their own "Bad Cop/ Good Cop" strategy to manage the staff. It developed naturally at first, but soon they intentionally played up their positions, each of which reflected their roles in my life as well as their personalities.

Playing their parts as the Bad Cop and the Good Cop each reinforced the other's image, which enhanced the staff's respect for both women. An employee might expect the patient's wife to be protective and stressed, so would understand if my wife was exacting and critical even if they didn't like it. But because she had raised such a sweet and devoted daughter, they came to also see her sympathetic and nurturing side. It was the reverse for my daughter's image. She may be a sweetie, but any daughter of that formidable wife must have a spine of steel, so they unquestioningly respected her authority.

Another factor bolstering my wife's credibility was her medical knowledge, including her familiar use of industry terms and jargon. This is a product of her decades doing ultrasound, nuclear medicine, and other imaging technologies in oncology, cardiology, and OB/GYN. It was more than just throwing the word "stat" into her conversation now and then. When she spoke, it was clear she knew what she was talking about.

I know she impressed the staff as a person to be reckoned with; I witnessed it. One night, after my wife had gone home after an earlier confrontation with an RT, the CNA and the LVN were in the room performing their evening duties. Neither one was involved in the blow-up, but they knew all about it. Neither were upset in any way themselves. They were discussing the incident, and the CNA mentioned she agreed with my wife that the tech had erred. Then, referring to my wife, she asked the nurse:

"Is she an M.D.?"

I was very proud. I smiled, inside.

"**G**ood morning, George."

I opened my eyes to see two images of Dr. Kumar leaning over the bed. I measured the distance between them, trying to determine if my double vision was improving. It seemed not as bad as on the day I became paralyzed.

I was about five weeks out of ICU and had been able to open my eyes for a few days. The right was mostly open but the left lagged, rising only halfway. They must have looked like a pair of windows with the shades pulled down to different heights. The sight of him was blurred as I normally wore glasses, and my eyes could not dilate or focus because the muscles that do that were still paralyzed, but I was glad I could finally see my doctor's face.

Dr. Kumar leaned his head back and peered at me. I recognized that movement; he wore bifocals. He took my hand in both of his, slipping one inside my grip to measure my strength, or more accurate, my weakness, and to detect my answers to his coming questions.

"Did you sleep well last night?"

I had rested as well as you'd expect in this hectic environment. I squeezed once.

"Is your wife coming to see you today?" Two squeezes.

"Will your daughter come?" One squeeze.

"Very good, George." He turned his head toward the ventilator and IV pumps; I saw bright blue flashes on his wireless spectacles, reflections of the machines' digital displays.

He went on to explain whatever the current situation and status was. His voice was warm and empathetic, but with a calm seriousness that projected authority.

Since his first visit when he lit a sort of fire within me to survive, everything I learned about this man was good. Everyone in the hospital described him only in the most admiring words. They all said the same things: he is one of the best pulmonologists in the area and always treats every single person – patients, family, nurses, and other staff – with the greatest respect and kindness. In the entire staff, I sensed their feelings toward him went beyond admiration to something like reverence.

This high esteem in which everyone held Dr. Kumar reminded me of my initial impression that he was in command of a healing power. Now that I knew more of his character, and since that power is an entirely good and beneficial thing, I came to consider it a holy power. What else can you call something that is focused purely on alleviating human suffering?

Putting that aspect of it aside, the power is real because of its demonstrated results. In me, the effect was to be physically energized and mentally renewed by an infusion of hope. In the staff, he inspired their best effort – whenever he asked someone to do something for me, they acted like they were on a mission of the utmost importance. I thought long and hard to understand this.

I saw that as a bird needs two wings to soar, there were

two sides to his greatness: He is a man of science and medicine, and one who recognizes the dignity and value of each person in every situation. His thirst for knowledge and drive for excellence have carried him to a high level professionally, but I believe his empathy is what motivates him in his work. Furthermore, his innate humane character makes him an effective leader for the staff, which makes for better care – and so, the healing power expands in ever-widening circles.

Taking into account Dr. Kumar's skill, compassion, and his effective leadership – all applied to furthering human health and life – I think here is an argument that his is a sacred gift.

A holy healing power – now, isn't that what you want in your doctor?

Spring was turning to summer. If there was a general recovery underway within this desiccated husk of a body, it was proceeding at a snail's pace.

All I could do was move my eyes and both eyelids. Keep my mouth a little less foolishly drooping open. I could flex my tongue and two fingers on one hand. My neck muscles were awakening a little, and I was starting to move my head. I tried shaking it to answer yes or no, but it came across as more of a wobble, and I had to continue using hand signals.

The main problem delaying improvement was limited lung capacity, which held down my blood oxygen level, which in turn reduced energy and slowed healing. In spite of Dr. Kumar's efforts, things were not going well. One reason was the hospital's lack of proper equipment. The previous hospital had a vibrating vest they put on me, driven by an air pump, which loosened the thicker fluids in my lungs so they could be suctioned away. This facility did not, so a significant level of congestion persisted. Someone said they once had a hand-held vibrating device that they held against the patient's chest, but no one could find it. Probably walked away.

Dr. Kumar and my wife both appealed to the insurance company to get a similar therapeutic vest, and they finally approved it. Inexplicably, even though it was bought specifically for me, the hospital purchased a size XL. It was too loose to do any good.

My wife expressed her frustration to the RT one night.

"He's had it a week and it doesn't seem to be helping at all. That was so stupid, getting him an extra-large. It would be perfect for somebody twice his size," she said with exasperation.

My RT, who was also the shift supervisor and very experienced, was pulling one of my hands through an armhole on the vest. "Yes," he replied, then paused with the vest halfway on me, staring at it, holding my hand in the air. "It's too bad it's not adjustable, like with straps or something. Some way to fit it around him."

He smiled. "Y'know, I think I have an idea," he said in a knowing tone. He went ahead and finished putting the vest on. It felt like a tent. He fiddled a moment with the loose-fitting material, pulling it tighter, then removed the vest and held it up.

"What if we take it in? Tailor it," he said. "We have a heavy-duty stapler in the RT office, so if I can sort of fold this over, there's this much excess material," he showed my wife his idea, "and put in a tight row of staples along here. That should hold the air. I'll be right back."

Soon he returned to show off his handiwork. He was excited.

"Okay, what do you think?" he asked.

"Looks great, I guess," my wife answered. "Will it work?"

"I tested it back in the office and no problem. Let me put it on him and let's see."

He leaned me forward and wrangled me into it, laid me back, and closed the front. I could feel it fit more like the other vests.

"Here goes," the RT sung out, and flipped the switch. I was immediately cocooned in the tight inflated vest, my body taken over by the pulsating waves of vibration that wiped out all other sensations, even any sense of time as long as it went on. In twenty minutes, he came back after helping another patient, took off the vest, and suctioned me.

I could tell by the deep vibrations that it had to be helpful. After suctioning, I was getting more air and was more comfortable.

After the RT was gone, my wife took my hand.

"Do you think that helped, honey?" One flex.

"Are you feeling like you have more capacity?" One flex.

"Good. You should start getting more oxygen now, at least a little more. But you're really only back where you were weeks ago," she fretted. "We missed all that time without the vest, all that time and no improvement . . . ." Her voice trailed off, leaving the room filled with the steady sound of air pushes from the ventilator.

There was one other option Dr. Kumar and the hospital were trying to pursue. We learned about it one morning when he came in with a woman we hadn't met before.

"Good morning, Mrs. Walsh," she greeted my wife, shaking her hand. "I'm Lyssa, the hospital director of respiratory therapy."

"Good morning, Mrs. Walsh," Dr. Kumar added. "Lyssa has a good suggestion we're trying to implement."

"Yes," Lyssa began, "there is a particular type of bed we'd like to acquire for Mr. Walsh, which is, ah, rather high tech.

The entire mattress can vibrate, at different settings and wave motions, depending on the patient's requirements, which loosen the deeper fluids so they can be removed more easily. It is much more therapeutic than the vest and will speed up his recovery. We can't do any more bronchoscopies; I understand your husband has already had three."

This surprised me. I had a vague memory of feeling better one evening and knowing I had a bronchoscopy but could not remember having any done – and it's an invasive procedure. The procedure involves the doctor inserting a flexible scope into the airway to examine the trachea and bronchi, as well as take specimens or, as in my case, do a deep suction. Now I find I had three and missed them all. It worried me that I needed so many.

My wife was pleased. "That vibrating bed would be great. I approve it," she said with a laugh. "Can we go ahead and order it?"

Lyssa sounded apologetic. "We already have put in a request with your insurance company, and are waiting to hear back. It is somewhat expensive, since it's not the standard hospital bed. We have told them he needs this, as the therapies we're using are inadequate to turn the tide."

Dr. Kumar cut in. "I have explained to them George is not progressing as I expected," he said earnestly, "and that he needs this new bed. I want you to know, Mrs. Walsh, and you, George, we will do everything we can to get this approved."

It was encouraging to hear a more therapeutic bed was available, but knowing the decision was in the hands of the insurance company rather than my doctor put a damper on the good news. I hoped the powers-that-be would agree with Dr. Kumar and Lyssa, and the sooner the better.

The simple problem of acquiring a relatively low-cost vibrating vest, much less buying a new high-tech hospital bed just for me, illustrated my unique status for the entire system. From the insurance bureaucracy to hospital management to the staff, including purchasing, nurses, therapists, and even Dr. Kumar, I was everybody's first botulism patient. I was a new textbook for them. My case was longer lasting, more complicated, and more confounding than anyone expected. Making their learning curve steeper was my severely weak and malnourished condition before I became paralyzed.

It is around this time I learned the name for my current condition: "quadriparesis." It means extreme weakness in all four limbs, or in my case, the entire body. This was what they were treating me for: quadriparesis secondary to botulism, "secondary" meaning resulting from and following another disease. The botulism was long over; it had done its worst – its absolute worst, short of killing me. The toxin had been neutralized, although too late to do me any good. Now, the enemy was my utter weakness, which could only be overcome by therapy to reconnect my brain to my body.

The task was formidable, even staggering in its scale: my body needed to remake millions and millions of nerve endings, new, healthy axons, one at a time, beginning at zero. It was dismaying to contemplate that what was wiped out in a few days would take years to rebuild. It seemed impossible it all could be restored.

The greatest worry looming over me was a non-stop terror: the ventilator breaks or the air tubes separate, help doesn't come in time, and I die – and this time I know what's going on and I'm watching it happen. Second worse was the reality of my existence: continual pain and discomfort, loss of dignity, disruption and destruction of my previous life – such as it was – combined with the prospect of a lengthy hospitalization. These critical concerns weighed on me incessantly, but sometimes even these were overwhelmed by a profound sadness at my isolation.

I had serious surgeries in the past and had felt vulnerable before, but this gulf dividing me from other people resulting from my inability to communicate was something I never experienced. Nor could I have imagined such frustration.

I had always been an informed and engaged patient, but in a situation enormously more complicated I could not be at all involved in helping manage my care. For example, I could not tell anyone if something went wrong with some equipment while they were gone, something that could be very serious. I could not give any feedback during a treatment or therapy to improve effectiveness or reduce pain. I could neither initiate an exchange nor convey any complex information.

Even with family at my bedside I felt terribly alone. I

hungered to make those simple everyday human connections – greeting someone, talking about the weather or the news. It hurt that I could not say, "Thank you," or "I love you."

My loneliness was particularly bitter one afternoon after I had been in considerable distress for a long time. When my wife came in, I was only able to make her understand I was suffering but wasn't in pain. My particular problem wasn't covered by her usual questions, and she could not guess what was wrong.

I felt a bitter blend of frustration and resignation building up inside me. It was a feeling I had become very familiar with. This was just one more of so many maddening and hopeless moments when I had no choice but to let it go. There was nothing I could do; I would have to endure until someone discovered the problem in the course of events, no matter how long that takes.

Then my wife had a brainstorm.

"Let's try this," she said. "I'll say the alphabet, and you squeeze when I get to the right letter. We'll spell it out. Okay? Okay.

"A – B – C – D . . . "

My mind was so dulled by the meds and I was so unaccustomed to concentrating, it took a few seconds to grasp the concept. Then I realized I actually needed to do something about it – work with and engage another person to solve a puzzle. I needed to think of what to say, to make it short, and spell it right. I felt under pressure; I had been in a completely passive role for almost three months, but now I was expected to perform.

I felt a sense of urgency as letter by letter the words emerged, not only so my wife could fix my problem quickly. I also felt a pent-up drive to connect with her. And despite being distressed by the problem, distracted by trying to concentrate on my spelling, and heavily medicated, I understood this was a very good idea and we will do this again.

As wonderful as our new spelling system was, it did have problems. It was slow and sometimes confusing. It was difficult for my wife to keep track of all the letters if the message was too long, after repeating almost the entire alphabet over and over. Sometimes I could not keep up with her pace and signaled too late, creating a typographical error. When that happened and a message turned bizarre, she would have to go back letter by letter so I could identify the mistake, and we'd start the rest of the message from there.

My daughter had her own technique and wrote down each letter. The string of letters created a kind of word puzzle, which she'd break down into a relevant phrase or sentence. By producing longer strings of words I could have almost normal, if short, conversations with her. I was excited the first time I got her to laugh using this system, which I confess was by making a snarky comment about someone on staff.

We soon developed ways to make it faster and more efficient. I would be asked, "Is it a vowel?" and if it was not, the next question was, "Is it in the first half of the alphabet?" and depending on my answer they would start with the appropriate letter. Within weeks, I took the initiative in counting to the right letter, which was more accurate and quicker.

My daughter suggested ways to improve my speed. If I gave a

long squeeze of the entire hand, the letter was a vowel, and I then flexed normally to select either A, E, I, O, U, or Y. If I squeezed my pinkie finger first, the next letter was in the second half of the alphabet and I began from that point. There was a wrinkle here, though: for some reason my wife began the second half of the alphabet with M, but my daughter started with N. Or vice-versa. I had to remember who used each version to avoid confusion.

I was grateful I could have a bit of conversation with my wife. Before she left me every evening, I would not let go of her hand until I let her know, "I-L-O-V-E-Y-O-U." Although she was exhausted and eager to leave, she usually humored me and let me finish.

I was also happy I could now initiate an exchange. If I wiggled my hand, and my wife or daughter were willing to pick it up, I was able to convey my thoughts when I wanted to.

One day my wife mentioned she had decided to hire a neighborhood handyman to paint our bedroom, a project I couldn't finish before the Crohn's flared up. She was going to exchange his time for our old van, which he had long wanted for his business, making the labor portion of the project cost-free.

As she told me this, I realized I could help. I had important information to share, and with our spelling system I had a way to share it. I felt excited that for the first time since I got sick, I had a chance to participate in life outside my hospital room.

Two years earlier we had redone the family room in what I consider a subtle pastel yellow; it is a very light shade and isn't even called a yellow in the name. Since we both really liked it, I bought extra so we could someday paint our bedroom the same shade. I never mentioned my idea to my wife, knowing she could always choose a different color when the time came.

If we were to use that paint, it would make the job completely free. I only had to tell her we had it. To make my message as short and as easy to sign as possible, I thought I should start with the "color" part before the "family room" part and tell her, "Use yellow from family room."

I wiggled my hand to talk. With my hand in hers I began. "U-S-E," then I paused.

"Use," my wife said.

I continued. "Y-E-L-L – "

She abruptly threw my hand down and said with disgust, "No way, Geo! I am not going to paint that room yellow! That would be so ugly! A yellow bedroom?!"

She must think I want a lemon yellow or some kind of gold, anything but the family room color. I waved my hand, wanting to finish my message, but she refused to pick it up.

She huffed and puffed for a few moments before continuing in an exasperated tone, "No. I'm going to use the same paint we used in the family room! We have plenty left over and I really like that color! And that way the whole job is free. Yellow? Gawd!"

I wanted to laugh but could only roll my eyes.

My world was very different with my eyes open again. My hearing was much less acute. I could no longer escape beyond the bed rail, spirited away by the sounds of a busy hospital. There were no more visions of the daily drama flying through my imagination – busy nurses in bright scrubs, the faces of staff and visitors passing by, the numbered doors and spare equipment in the halls, the gleaming surfaces and calming decor of an idealized modern healthcare facility.

Instead, my colorful hospital reality show was replaced by grim reality. Without my eyeglasses and with my paralyzed pupils fully dilated, the entire scene was an indistinct collage of gray and beige blurs. The head of the bed was always raised to a thirty-degree angle, and because I could not turn my head, I was stuck in a fixed position facing straight forward. My view was restricted to little more than the wall in front of me.

Looking across the wall, first I could see the right half or so of white floor-to-ceiling cabinets, the rest obscured by a wall on my left. Next, a sink jutting from the wall with a mirror over it, exposed plumbing below; a paper towel dispenser; a fixture holding boxes of latex gloves. Over the gloves was the round shape of a clock, its face a blank as I could not see its hands or numbers.

Directly in front was a small table where the LVNs mixed

the medicines they injected into my G-tube. Then the sharps disposal, wipes dispenser, dark gray medicine cabinet, and a stand-up computer station built onto the wall. Above the computer hung the black, blocky shape of a television. Last was the wipe board where they wrote the day, date, and names of my nurses; I could not see the lettering.

On the corridor wall the door was usually wide open; on the large window facing the nurses' station the blinds were typically down but open. Under the window sat a square-framed armchair of dark wood and dirty blue fabric.

On the right in the corner of my eye was the IV pole rigged with three pumps, but I could not lift my head to see the bags of saline, meds, and TPN hanging above. On my chest were a few white air tubes connected to a square box and two translucent blue air hoses running out of sight to the ventilator.

Depending on whether I felt hot or cold, I was covered with some combination of faded blue patient gown, dull white sheet, and ivory-colored knitted blanket. I was penned in by bed rails of healthcare beige.

The forlorn and alienating character of this tableau was multiplied by my double vision. It was getting better but still persisted.

This was my world, because on my left was a blank gray wall. This was the wall of the bathroom, the door of which opened away from me toward those white cabinets. This room's layout, with the bathroom on the exterior wall, put the window around the corner from me – I could not see the window itself, much less the sky, the trees, the sunsets.

So, to me, the "outside" was outside my door, where throughout the day, nurses and therapists, people moving carts, patients pushing walkers, family members, and white-coated doctors and techs passed by, each for only a second. A single glimpse was an intriguing video clip from the story of someone else's life, a reminder of freedom and precious commonplace occurrences. I was jealous. Lying there helpless, I was the still point in the center of my universe while the world spun on without me.

My days were foggy and dim; the nights were too bright. I was becoming more wakeful, even during the night, when it was blatantly obvious I was living in somebody else's 24/7 workspace. In past hospitalizations, to make my room quieter and more restful at night, I always asked for the door to be closed and I'd cover the lighted face of the IV pump with a washcloth. Now, the several digital screens on the pumps and respirator bathed me in their cyan glow that washed across the bed curtain on my right, the ceiling above, and the wall on my left. Inside this claustrophobic grotto, I could only stare ahead at the angled shards of cold light from the hallway streaming through the door and window blinds, falling across the darkened wall in front of me.

Increased wakefulness was a sign of improvement, but the downside was having more time to think. Every minute of the day reminded me what a nightmare I inhabited. I was frustrated that even though it had been three months since I fell ill, I was still only beginning recovery. Beyond that, it all seemed almost pointless. All of it. I didn't want to die but I presumed this herculean effort to save me would only bring forth a severely diminished life – I'd be bedridden or, if lucky, wheelchair bound.

There was nothing good to think about and too much time to think it. Time became a sort of enemy, or at least a barrier. Time was an endless, bottomless sea between me and a distant shore.

I felt very low then, to awaken into all this. I wondered what the effect of the anti-depressives were on keeping me from despair or panic. Not that there was anything I could do about it; I was unable to reach over and switch off the ventilator. In addition, there were all these smiling people coming in, helping and encouraging me, bound and determined to keep me alive, whose works were carrying me along downstream regardless of my final destination. It would be wrong to let them down.

That was when I remembered some news I received just before the botulism struck. During the two weeks after my victory over Crohn's, I worked on updating my résumé and refreshing professional contacts. One day I was surprised to find an unopened email from a former colleague that was sent fourteen months earlier. She had asked me to join her network a few weeks before, and then we bounced a few messages back and forth to catch up.

Because each message was a reply to the first, they all had the same subject line, "Please join my network," each with one more "RE:" in front of it. She sent it when my Crohn's was turning very bad and I was dropping out of the business world, and with the repetitive title it was easy to overlook. The dull subject line gave me no clue of the shocking news inside.

She was writing – again, over a year earlier – to let me know a man we had both worked for had just died from a sudden, massive heart attack. He was only a few years older than me, and I admired him for his success and character. I felt terrible I didn't see this message in time to have reached out to his family or attend a memorial.

But worse was the realization that he and I both faced a health crisis at about the same time, and I was able to fight back while he never had a chance. He accomplished so much more than me – why had he been taken while I was still here? It didn't make sense. I decided to write his son, who was also his business partner, but the botulism stopped me a few days later.

Now, my former colleague's bad news came back to haunt me. Most often it happened at night when, unable to sleep, my mind worked on the unwritten letter over and over, drafting and revising it. Unable to write or use a computer, I could not finish it so I could resolve neither my sadness for his passing, nor my confusion and humility over being spared. These feelings were sharpened by the added knowledge that while he did not have even one chance to fight back, I had now been given two.

Night after night I pondered this mystery as I lay immersed in the icy blue glow of digital displays. I was grateful to be alive and regretted all I lost, but that seemed inadequate considering he lost everything.

Thinking of him, I began to better understand the value of time, and I came to see there are two sides to time. There's time in the big-picture sense – the future. That was out of my hands. I could not bring it on; I could only prepare to meet it.

This thought that I was preparing for my future made me appreciate the other side of time: time on the smaller scale – how we experience life as a series of ephemeral, singular moments. I understood I had only so many moments, and no more, and to optimize my recovery I had to fill every single one with as much work and effort as I could.

I realized I was wrong to think time was only an obstacle; time is also a tool, and I was going to use it.

Part Four

I love fireworks for their intense colors, the impact of the explosion, the delight of the dramatic finale. This Fourth of July, I could only see ghosts of fireworks flickering on my wall of white cabinets, displayed as patches of pale colors projected from somewhere outside my window. I could hear their detonations, muted in here, but felt nothing. I thought of the people there looking up at a sky full of wonder as the show rose to its crescendo.

While watching this, I noticed an odd thing. Although these faded flashes of color travelled upwards on the wall, their rising actually tracked the firework's downward path in its brief moments of power and light.

A few weeks after I could open my eyes, my neck muscles also started to revive. I began to do head exercises, repeatedly pressing it back into the pillow, turning it left and right, and tilting it up and down. No longer locked into a thrown-back position, my head hung heavy, but I could look about me a bit. I could make my meaning clear when I shook my head "yes" or "no."

My hands continued to improve as well, and I could finally use the call button. Until now, even if the device was put in my hand and my finger placed right on the button – even a special soft-touch device for very weak patients – I could not make it connect. Being cut off from help during another life-threatening crisis had been one of my greatest worries.

Now that I could push the button when needed, I felt relief, and a sense of control. Using our alphabet system, I asked for the hallway window blinds to be shut and the door closed most of the time, both at night and during the day. I was still nervous to be out of sight in case there was an emergency, but I felt I was ready to put a shield between me and the unending mania outside my room.

The call button was also the television remote control, but my eye problems made watching TV uncomfortable. My double vision was almost resolved, but the eye injury I suffered over two months earlier wasn't healed. The constant stinging had faded, but I still felt a painful scratching with every blink, and the eye turned red and gooey. I had conjunctivitis, which also spread to my left eye.

Making this worse, the *C. botulinum* toxin had dried up my tear ducts as it had my salivary glands. Without normal lubrication, already inflamed, and continually exposed to dehumidified indoor air, both eyes were itchy, crusted over, hot, and dry.

There was no specialist on staff to address any issues specific to the eyes, so these problems could not be treated, including the injury, even after I was able to communicate about it. Dr. Kumar prescribed moisturizing eye drops, but I could never get them as frequently as I wanted. When they finally did come, it was a welcome relief to feel the warm, damp cloth on my eyelids, the nurse swabbing away the scratchy granulated discharge, and then the cool, soothing drops going in.

Since I was now awake more of the day, I decided I needed to exercise my brain. I felt I must do something to stay sharp and take my mind off this grinding boredom and fear, like work on some sort of puzzle. I started by adding up our monthly family budget, trying to remember each item, and keep the calculation clear enough for long enough to come to a sum. It was okay if I lost track or came up with different answers, the point was to keep thinking logically.

In my current circumstances, however, money was a troubling subject, so I switched to sports. I tried to remember all the teams by name and city in all the major sports, and then by their division and conference. And then do it again. I tried to recall the playoff contestants and league champions in each year working back in time, but my memory was almost blank. Funny, that; it all seemed so important at the time.

Drip by drip, the days accumulated. I progressed only gradually and got stuck in a frustrating pattern of two steps forward and one step back. Usually the problem was an infection; I was often fighting UTIs and upper respiratory infections including several bouts with pneumonia. When I was sick I didn't have the energy to get therapy, setting back my schedule and taking away some hard-earned gains.

One day my wife bought in a small CD player so I could have some music. Usually the only time I got to enjoy it was when either she or my daughter put a disk on when they left for the night. I certainly couldn't run it, and the staff didn't have time. It helped me fall asleep, listening to John and Paul, or George Bizet. For me, hearing music again was like coming upon an oasis in the desert.

Sometimes, while I drifted asleep listening to it, my imagination would take over and create intriguing visions. Perhaps from exhaustion, isolation, and the narcotics, my mind's eye would see each piece of music as a sort of mechanical device, a type of motor, with its numerous parts moving in precise, coordinated actions. This engine existed in a dark void, and the movable elements were fashioned of neon lights. The parts of this complex apparatus were the notes and instruments and voices, and they would extend in and out, rotate and unfold in rhythmic patterns. The separate actions would become more elaborate, the parts would execute more intricate variations as the song peaked. I thought I had discovered some secret behind the mystery of music.

I was fascinated. The music would fill my head and I'd study that mesmerizing musical engine built of light and color and sound, a machine made of fireworks.

The paralysis seemed to be receding from the top down. First my eyes and tongue, then the eyelids and neck began to reactivate, which meant I was ready to start speech therapy.

The first thing I learned in speech therapy is the tongue is the only muscle in the body that is not attached at both ends. This is significant because that makes it harder to exercise. Rachel, my therapist, explained this while teaching me drills that would help me eventually eat and swallow, and speak once more. I worked at them throughout the day and often at night. Even if I never walked again, at least I wanted to be able to eat and talk.

One day speech therapy gave me a glimpse of that future when Rachel brought in a special device.

In her early thirties, I guessed, with light brown hair, light-colored eyes and a friendly personality, Rachel was quite talkative. I thought it was good my speech therapist liked to talk and wondered if it was a qualification for the job. She was knowledgeable and informative, and mostly serious. Sometimes, however, her enthusiasm for her work and youthful exuberance bubbled up through the professional surface.

"This," she said cheerily, taking a small tube from a flat round container, "is your new speaking valve." She held it up, turned it back and forth, and tilted her head, smiling. "It is called a PMV, for Passy-Muir Valve. This little guy is not only going to let you talk, but is going to be, like, so important for improving your diaphragm," she explained, nodding for emphasis.

"It is so cool. It was invented by a guy who was actually on a ventilator himself. He was disabled, muscular dystrophy I believe, and eventually had to be ventilated and couldn't talk anymore. So, he's stuck in a wheelchair and he's probably like all, 'What can I do while I'm just sitting here?' right? Well, first, he was depressed, but he turned his frustration into an idea that helped, gosh – maybe millions? – of people. True story.

"Okay. The way the PMV works is, it's a one-way valve. It lets air in but not out. It changes the way you exhale. It makes you exhale, actually. Instead of the ventilator pulling air out through the trach, the patient has to exhale. The valve forces the air to go up through your throat in the normal way. That allows you to talk." She concluded on an up note, but added in a rapid stream of words, "Although it will be pretty limited for you until you have more force and better articulation.

"More important for you than talking – is – since the patient initiates the exhalation, it exercises the diaphragm. And as I mentioned, that is so important because of the damage from the botulism. You've been on full vent support for so long the muscle has like zero strength now," she added sadly.

"So that being said, today, by starting you on the PMV, is actually the first step in weaning you off the ventilator," she announced, back to her normal upbeat tone.

She leaned forward to take the air hose off my tracheostomy, attach the PMV to the trach, and reconnect the air supply.

"There you go. Per-fect," she said, low in her throat. "I just have to deflate the cuff." She used a syringe to release the air that kept my lungs sealed off from my mouth. "And now, the air can go out through your throat, over the vocal cords. As in – talking?"

She stood back. Her eyes lit up in anticipation; her smile looked eager, playful. I didn't know what to do.

"Try to talk," she urged.

"Ahhh, ahhh." My voice was raspy and almost inaudible. Feeling vibrations in my throat felt strange and distracted me from trying to make sense. I didn't know what to say anyway. "Awk. Awk now. Ty to taw. Can taw now, I talk. Wha 'ould I 'ay?"

I was amazed to hear a sound come out of me, and I could hardly articulate any words. My tongue was sluggish but my lips and face felt frozen – they had been paralyzed too, and this was the first time they moved since that day. Rachel began asking me questions to keep me vocalizing and working. Her energy made it fun, but I was surprised how much effort it took. After only ten minutes I was exhausted and my lower chest felt sore. I realized using the PMV was serious exercise.

The PMV was an exciting revelation. It gave me back the power of speech, though for now it would only be offered in tiny slices, a few minutes at a time, a few days each week. I took this as a breakthrough and hoped the ability to connect normally with other people was not too far over the horizon.

Just as the myriad rhythms of the seas are ordered by the daily tides, the cycles of life in the hospital come to a turning point twice each day at change of shift. Confined to my bed across the hallway from the nurses' station, I was a close witness to these occurrences. Each began a little after six-thirty when a rising surge of sound filled my room with an increasing din of more and more voices, with more intensity, reaching its highest point just before seven. The roar of this human wave crested at that level for perhaps an hour as all the RNs, LVNs, and CNAs get patient updates from their counterparts and discuss new orders or emergent issues, and each one is either charting and reporting or planning and organizing their shift.

During this time, the staff is more turned inward toward themselves and away from patient care. Of course, no one merely stops handling an ongoing or urgent situation, but it was normal for me to not get a staff visitor from just after six until well after eight. This was the case morning and night, but it was worse in the evening. Then, when people were livelier and louder, with personal greetings and conversations adding to the buzz of shop talk, it was not a good time to get something if you needed it quickly.

So, at one evening's change of shift, it was the very worst

time for the air hose to slip off my tracheostomy, disconnecting me from the respirator.

There were many places it could have separated. The two blue tubes from the respirator met at one junction box, then a single white tube went to a four-way connector, which fit onto the actual tracheostomy. That night, it was the connection between the single tube and the four-way that slipped apart – just when the staff was most preoccupied.

What first caught my attention was a new sound: steady breaths of air going out the end of the tube, into the room, not into my lungs. I looked down, and on the edge of my vision below my chin was the loose hose laying on my chest. My eyes popped open. I pressed the call button. I knew all those people out there were busy but, I told myself, *someone is sure to look in on me, very soon.*

I realized that since I was keeping my door and blinds closed, looking in on me wasn't as easy as it was. Before, someone could merely turn their head to see I had an emergency in here, but saving me today would take more effort. I wanted privacy and quiet; now I wished I were still on display.

I considered what a diver or astronaut would do; I tried to stay calm to conserve energy and reduce my need for oxygen. I hoped it was a good thing my metabolism was low and I was so thin. *I don't need much.*

I could only move my arms below the elbow, so couldn't simply put the hose back on. With my fingertips I was able to loosely grasp a part of the tube laying on my belly, several inches from the separation. *Very soon now, very soon they'll come.* I tried to push the loose end back toward the connector, hoping to hold the ends together until help arrived. My clumsy fingers fumbled with it; I could maneuver it closer but I couldn't see what I was doing or feel the ends touch. Then I changed hands so I could press the call button again. And press it again and again. I was getting nervous.

I couldn't understand why someone hadn't looked in. *Didn't they see I signaled all these times?* That's what I imagined: each press of the button made a light flash and a buzzer sound on some board at the nurses' station, and with all those repeated signals they must realize this is an emergency. In reality, there are two lights, one above my door and one at the station, which turn on and slowly flash, and no buzzer sounds the alarm. When those lights start blinking there is no way for anyone to know the difference between "I need ice water" and "I need air."

I squinted at the clock but couldn't see the hands. It felt to me that more than a minute had already passed with no response. I was upset no one could be bothered to take two steps, open the door, and glance inside. Meanwhile, the sound outside the room was growing louder as the hour approached. Suddenly the noise boomed and the crowd got almost boisterous. Someone must have come back from a vacation or a wedding because I heard loud calls like, "How'd that go?" and "Let me tell you!" and "Oh my god!" People were laughing!

I was getting furious – and panicky. *What's taking them so long? Can't they see I'm not kidding?* Contemplating dying from a simple accident after all I've been through, while help is out there – *right there!* – filled me with a bitter sadness pushing away my anger and fear.

I started pressing the call button over and over. They must see it now! *It's got to be almost five minutes!*

Finally, the door swung open and the excitement and energy of the crowd flooded the room. Leaning in on the door handle quite casually was one of the day shift CNAs, smiling as if still enjoying whatever cute story someone was telling out there. I waved the loose air tube, my eyes begging for help.

"Yes, Mr. Walsh? What do –? Oh, look at you!" She frowned slightly but her smile didn't change. She calmly came over to the bed, took the tube from me and slipped it on the four-way connector. I felt my chest inflate.

"There you go. Don't worry, you weren't in danger. You're monitored." She smiled wider and stepped back, hands clasped in front of her.

"Was that all?" she asked.

I nodded "yes." My eyes were as big as saucers. *Was that all?!*

"Would you like your door closed?"

I hesitated, then shook my head "no."

"Alright. Good night, Mr. Walsh," she sang out, turning away. The waves of sound washed around the room and the hospital went on as if nothing had happened.

I was stunned and relieved but dismayed she was so cavalier about the whole thing. I promised myself right then that if I ever put this episode down in writing it would be one of the greatest examples of indifferent and endangering "care" I was subjected to. Then I realized the important thing isn't what happened, it's what did not happen. I did not die or pass out. I did not get dizzy. I don't recall feeling short of breath.

I couldn't explain why. Perhaps I got the tube close enough to the connector to get me some air, just enough. I probably began this episode with a high blood oxygen saturation, which may have helped. I also wondered if the handful of PMV therapy sessions I had by then were enough to give me a slight ability to breathe on my own.

But I knew what the CNA said was accurate: I was monitored, so I was never in danger. If I had gotten into real trouble, the pulse/ox, heartbeat, and respiratory alarms would have gone off and assistance would have arrived in seconds. I hoped.

This crisis, or what I thought was a crisis, demonstrated how important it was to liberate me from the ventilator. As long as I was on full support, and the machine was breathing for me, my diaphragm wouldn't get enough work to rebuild its nerve connections. Working with the PMV wasn't enough; the next step was to force me to take complete breaths.

This is done by changing the respirator's support mode to CPAP, for continuous positive airway pressure. CPAP provides a steady pressure but requires the patient to initiate each breath. I didn't think I could do it. I was scared to try. But the therapists wanted me to start and pointed out I had to do it sometime. I also knew, just as I found with my eyes and tongue and hands, there was no alternative to just doing the work.

One day, my RT was a guy we called "Mountain Man," a burly fellow with a bushy beard and a wide, friendly smile. He brought up CPAP again and encouraged me to try it.

"I told you before, you have to start sometime," he said with a shrug. "What do you say we do it now? I promise to come back immediately if you experience any distress."

He looked toward my daughter sitting on the other side of the bed. "If he gets in trouble, you can come find me and drag me back. Okay?"

She agreed. That made me feel safer, so after four months of full support I agreed to let him change the ventilator over to CPAP.

I'm sure he understood how frightening this was for me, for any patient. It's a big step in the weaning process. The very idea brought up terrifying memories of my close encounter with death. My stress rose when he turned toward the ventilator. I felt a change when he switched off full support but couldn't tell if I had more air or less. I could sense by the stillness in my lungs that air wasn't moving. He turned back, his face calm, his eyes reassuring.

"Good luck, Mr. Walsh. I will be back soon," he said, and walked away.

I started feeling short of breath within moments of his leaving, and it quickly grew worse. I lasted all of forty-five seconds before I sent my daughter to go find him. I was gasping and sweating when he returned. I was on CPAP for a maximum of three minutes, but it seemed like an hour. It would have been difficult enough, but I panicked as well, making it even harder to tolerate. I was embarrassed to have done so poorly and figured the RT had to be disappointed in me too. While he reset the machine, I hung my head and wouldn't look at him.

"Mountain Man" wasn't having any of my regrets.

"No worries, Mr. Walsh," he boomed cheerily. "The important thing is, you started. It doesn't matter how you started, you started. Alright, dude!" I looked up; he was beaming. I believe he would have high-fived me if I was able to lift my arm. I couldn't laugh but smiled in spite of myself.

That difficult first attempt was the start of a frustrating process. Even several weeks after starting CPAP, I could tolerate only three hours each day spread over several sessions. This was far below Dr. Kumar's expectations. My times were actually declining at that point, and I was having difficulty tolerating CPAP at all.

I decided to use my new tool, the speaking valve, to talk this over with him. I thought if I explained my sensations it might help him find a solution to my lack of progress. Rachel was always suggesting I use the valve with visitors, not only to chat but to get more exercise, but I hadn't yet. I now felt strong enough, and had an important enough reason, to try it. Early the next morning, pointing to the trach and pantomiming "talk" with my hands, I asked the day shift RT to put it on.

Dr. Kumar's usually placid face changed to a slight smile when he walked in the door. He must have noticed the speaking valve and was pleasantly surprised. I hoped he was also impressed I was being proactive about my care by using the PMV; it was obvious I did this to communicate with him. He stood at the side of the bed.

"Good morning, George," he said with a tone of expectation.

"Good morning, Doctor," I replied in a raspy whisper. This was the first time I spoke to him in the four months and longer I had been his patient. There was so much I wanted to say to him, but there was no time and not enough breath in me if there were. I stuck to the business at hand.

"CPAP's not getting better. I feel it's not filling my lungs. Not a complete breath," I explained.

Dr. Kumar asked me a few questions and was able to understand what I was experiencing.

"I am glad you had them put the valve on to talk to me," he said. "It is very helpful. I will try increased pressure support. I will put in the order now; the RT will make the adjustments. You should feel better afterward." He smiled down at me. "Have a good day, George."

I looked into his eyes. "Thank you, Doctor."

Saying those three words felt like the release of a mighty flood that had been dammed up inside me.

Our talk resulted in rapid improvement. The increased pressure made me more comfortable and within the week I was again extending my times on CPAP.

Second to breathing on my own, getting back on my feet was the most important challenge I faced. I set a goal to eventually be able to transfer myself from the bed to a wheelchair so I wouldn't be a complete burden on my wife or be trapped in bed the rest of my life. Before I could attempt anything like that, however, there was much work to do. Phase one was to get used to being upright again. We take it for granted in our normal lives, as we are sitting, walking, or standing most of the time, but I had lost that basic capability.

Kate, one of my two regular physical therapists, explained. "If we sit you up on the side of the bed or in a chair, you'll pass out. After all this inactivity, plus the wasting and malnutrition from Crohn's, your heart is weaker, and you don't have the muscle mass or muscle tone to help maintain your BP either."

To prepare me for being upright, Dr. Barone's team applied three techniques. The first I called "The Chair of Torture." It was a bare metal frame with a bicycle-style seat without a cushion and an upper-body wire cage to hold the patient in a slight reclining position. With zero padding on me and a bed sore, sitting on the hard seat was excruciating. I always tipped over inside the cage, and my bones would press painfully against the unforgiving metal bands. I likened it to a medieval dungeon's Iron Maiden.

The two aides who handled that duty showed little concern for my fragile condition. They were always in a hurry, and manhandled me into the device before rushing off to other duties. It was physically agonizing, and I was frustrated because I couldn't communicate to correct or guide them. Using our alphabet system, I informed my wife that it hurt. Once she saw for herself how rough it was, she stopped that therapy going forward.

The next method was the tilt table, one of Kate's specialties. Kate had a sharp, sometimes sarcastic sense of humor, shoulder-length blond hair parted toward the side, and stylish oversized dark-framed glasses. She was maybe fifteen years younger than us but had a grown child, and related well with both my wife and daughter. She was the kind of person you'd want as a neighbor or co-worker, someone you liked and trusted.

The first few times we worked together, however, she ticked me off. She seemed to have a rather nonchalant attitude toward the severity of my condition. I respected her experience but thought she didn't appreciate my case was unique, or didn't really care.

I began to understand her way of thinking when she came in for a session one day after I had missed several with an infection.

"It's a shame you had this delay in your PT," she began. "It's like you take two steps forward and then one step back –" She stopped herself short. She tilted her head and cracked a sly smile, like a light went off in her head. "No," she said emphatically. "It's not a step back. It's a step sideways. Yeah, sideways. Not back. Right?" She looked very pleased with herself. Raising her eyebrows and nodding at me, she asked again, more insistently, "Right?"

I nodded back.

"And you're not going backwards anyway, really," she added, tossing away the idea with a dismissive, one-shoulder shrug. I started to like her brand of positive thinking.

The tilt table was like a narrow ping pong table. Kate and an aide would slide me onto it, strap me down, and then she'd rotate it so my feet went down and my head went up. During the session she continually checked my blood pressure and oxygen saturation, and many times low readings cut the session short. We started at a very shallow angle and gradually raised it over several weeks. Progress was slow, but my heart responded to the increased work until I could tolerate a steep angle for forty-five minutes.

Since I was inactive during this PT therapy, it allowed the OT to work with me during the same session as well. This scheduling flexibility helped them save time. It was also a benefit to me, because my PT Kate and OT Laurie were good friends, and I enjoyed their animated conversations.

One day, however, the discussion turned a little dark. Laurie was working on my shoulder at the time.

"Oh, oh, Kate. Hey, did you ever hear any of the rumors about ghost sightings at our other facility?"

"Ha!" Kate exclaimed. "I think I heard a thing or two. Why?"

Laurie's eyes widened. "Well, I used to work there, and I heard lots of stories. Apparently, sometime in the past, years before we took it over, some weird things happened there to patients. Bad things. I used to work over there, and people told me some pretty bizarre things.

"And it happened to me one time. I was in the therapy office, which is on the first floor, and it has just a few skinny windows that go all the way down to the floor, you know?"

"Yeah, I've been there," Kate interjected. "Meetings."

"Oh, sure. Well, I'm doing a report at a desk right next to one of those windows, and out of the corner of my eye I see something moving outside, low to the ground, and it stops right there. I can tell it's a face, but I look up at the room, wondering, hoping I didn't really see this. Then, when I look back, it's gone! And something had definitely been there the second before! Girl, my heart was pounding!"

"Oh, God, that's creepy!" Kate squealed with excitement.

"Yeah, but the creepiest thing was what a patient saw," Laurie continued. "And it wasn't just once."

I didn't like where this was going.

"Well, one of my friends who's still there told me something that happened, oh, maybe a year ago. A patient, a man, reported that for several nights in a row, in the middle of the night, he saw a ring of ghostly spirits flying around his room above his bed." She paused and raised her eyebrows. "Ghosts, circling above the bed, night after night," she intoned.

"Ooh, I can just see it!" Kate shuddered with pleasure, giggling.

Laurie didn't look at me while telling the story, so she didn't see my eyes as wide as saucers and the worried look on my face.

Later, in my darkened room, surrounded by the eerie blue

glow of digital displays, I couldn't help but think of the other patient's ghastly vision and imagine a circle of restless, departed spirits swirling over me. I did not sleep well that night.

The last technique to get me acclimated to being upright was also the simplest: sitting up on the side of the bed.

Marielle, my other regular physical therapist, handled this. A slight woman with jet black hair pulled back into a long pony tail, she had a wide smile and warm brown eyes brimming with encouragement. Marielle was born overseas, and despite a difficult life, she became stronger, not harder. She had a sweet but stoic personality that helped me stay focused on the moment and kept me working hard.

One morning, after coming in and saying hello, Marielle faced me with a cheery smile. "At our meeting today, Doctor Barone and the PT staff agree you're ready to try sitting up on the side of the bed." I was surprised; this was a significant change. I was apprehensive and glad Marielle was with me for this.

She brought a chair next to the head of the bed. "You're going to do so well," she added in a musical voice, as if encouraging one of her small children.

"First of all, I have to lower the bed." My head and knees went down until I was lying flat. "Then let down the rail." She bent down and released the catch. I felt and heard the thud when it hit bottom. Although I was staring at the ceiling I could feel the increased space to that side. For over four months, there had always been a barrier inches from my head; now the wall was far away. Sensing this unfamiliar emptiness frightened me.

As if answering my thoughts, Marielle said, "You know, Mr. Walsh, when I sit you up on the side of the bed, I think it's probably the first time you won't be constrained since you got sick. Don't worry. You won't be on your own. I'll be within arm's reach, sitting right here. I'm not going to let you fall."

"Now I'll turn you onto your right side." She rolled me over, and I felt a shortness of breath as my chest collapsed, squeezing my lungs.

"And . . . bring your legs over the side." It was strange to feel my legs simply sticking out in the air again.

She took hold of my shoulders. "Now, I'm going to bring you up," she said matter-of-factly, and in a single movement swung my body from laying down to fully upright. I was disoriented by the sudden rotation of the room spinning before my eyes. At first, I thought it was the room moving, not me.

Then Marielle let go and sat down. I was on my own.

The air was cool on my feet and the bed rail cold against the back of my calves. My hands could not get a firm grip on the edge of the bed; my stiff fingers clawed at the sheets. I looked down at the blurred gray void beyond my knees and wobbled, a little dizzy. It was like sitting on a ledge atop a tall building.

My shoulders were hunched, and my head hung over my chest. I realized with alarm I was top-heavy and recognized the worst possible scenario: falling straight forward onto my face. I visualized – could almost feel – the floor rushing toward me, my arms moving up helplessly, my head whipping down against the hard tile. My heart raced with fear as I teetered on the brink.

"Head up!" Marielle called.

I jerked my chin up. I felt more balanced, and was surprised to find I was looking out the hallway window.

After all this time in one fixed position with one constant view, I was startled to look at something different and to see out so far. I couldn't see much, just indistinct glimpses of the heads and shoulders of people standing at the nurses' station, and beyond that a few open doorways to other patient rooms.

I stared out, and a sad thought came to me: I was looking into the past. Seeing just a sliver of normal life filled me with longing to rejoin the real world, yet it seemed distant, unreal, forever out of reach. This was hard to take. Feeling that sharp yearning for normality was more difficult and exhausting than the physical challenge.

I pressed my knuckles into the bed and steadied myself.

Since I was able to understand what happened to me, a crucial question hovered in the back of my mind: what was going on with my intestines and Crohn's disease while I'm paralyzed?

There was reason to hope the disease had not flared again. I had just undergone successful surgery before I was hit with botulism, and after previous surgeries for Crohn's I had enjoyed a period of good health. But stress is often a trigger for Crohn's, and being suddenly paralyzed and almost dying creates enormous stress. It was possible the illness was very active. We had no way of knowing.

Nevertheless, getting my intestines immobilized so soon after severe illness and major surgery must be having some effect on them. Was it good or bad?

One thing that worried me was whether post-surgical scar tissue was still forming when I became paralyzed and continued afterward. Scarring can sometimes adhere the intestine to the abdominal wall, and these lesions can keep the bowel from moving around to accommodate digestion. If I had formed lesions, it was also possible part of my intestine was locked in a too-tight turn, there may be a kink in the hose. Such a narrowing would be a built-in obstruction and require immediate major surgery, and we'd only discover it when I eat again.

On the other hand, this inactivity might be the perfect vacation for my guts. Maybe a long rest was just what they needed, and they'll recuperate better this way. I thought how ironic it would be if contracting botulism was a lucky break, as far as my Crohn's was concerned.

Despite detecting no signs of motility, in late July Dr. Kumar hoped my intestines were ready to absorb tube feeding. In tube feeding, a liquified food would be pumped directly into my stomach through the G-tube. This formula provided better nutrition than TPN. If I could tolerate it and absorb enough nourishment, they would be able to take out the picc line. I looked forward to having one less hole in me, especially that particular hole, one of my most serious infection risks.

The changeover started well. Within two weeks they removed the picc line. It was a gruesome sight but a good sensation to feel that long bloody tube slithering out of my upper arm. Unfortunately, like every other aspect of my treatment, this did not sail forward on a straight and steady course. Within days, I stopped absorbing the new food, and they had to put in another picc line.

One piece of good fortune for me at this hospital was the GI doctor on staff happened to be my long-time physician, Dr. Sinha. He didn't have much involvement early on, but now started working more closely with Dr. Kumar. His fix was to switch my G-tube to a G-J tube. This is a tube-within-a-tube: the wider and shorter G-tube into the stomach is for gastric suction; inside it is the narrower and longer J-tube extending into the jejunum for medications and feeding. Dr. Sinha's solution worked, and in another two weeks they took out the picc line again.

At times the outlet of the J-tube got plugged by particles of crushed pills or loose time-release pellets. Until the blockage was cleared, they couldn't get any meds in, and I could not be fed. Sometimes a hard push cleared the jam, but pushing too hard could burst the tube. For the most stubborn blockages, one of the more experienced nurses had a trick. She'd inject a small amount of a carbonated cola beverage and wait a half-hour. It worked very well, and they had to resort to this remedy several times. Unfortunately, there were occasions it could not be cleared and Dr. Sinha had to replace the entire G-J device.

Upgrading from IV nutrition to tube feeding brought up an issue I had not dealt with in more than five months. Once food was going into my intestines, something was sure to come out – just by gravity, even without bowel motility – which meant I needed to be cleaned up down there several times a day.

I'd push the call button. Eventually someone would look in.

"Yes, Mr. Walsh?" I'd point at my midsection.

"Oh, you need a clean-up?" I'd shake my head.

"Okay, I'll tell your CNA."

In time, the CNA came, always friendly, usually chatty. They'd lower the side rail and pull the blanket off. I'd feel the cool room air on my legs and look down at them, pale and thin, shin bones knife-sharp. The head of the bed would go down until I was staring at the ceiling, which then came closer as the bed was elevated. Practiced hands would take my shoulder and hip and turn me on my side while a weird sideways panorama rolled by – from ceiling, bed curtains, IV pole and pumps to the inside of the bed rail. I'd feel the discomforting compression on my lungs as my loosely bundled bones collapsed into this new configuration.

The CNA's small talk helped me block out what was happening. My eyes wandered over the details of things I could only see at times like this: the lettering and serial numbers on the IV pumps, the rippled reflection of light on the hanging bags, the faithful ventilator with its cold blue numbers and the steady pattern of its moving yellow line.

I'd try not to think of what I was feeling – embarrassment, shame, anger – over this new kind of loss, perhaps the loss of adulthood. But I was grateful every time. I tried to always keep in mind how lucky I was that in such an impersonal and often dehumanizing environment, I had someone to help me with such a primal human need.

I was staring at the door. My pulse quickened when I saw a shadow appear on the blinds and the handle turn. It was my nurse, Daniel, as I hoped. My eyes locked on what he was holding: a packaged syringe kit and the ampule of Dilaudid.

"I got your pain shot, Geo," he said. His voice was reassuring, his face calm.

He put the kit and ampule on the bed next to my legs, then stepped over to the wall for a moment to grab and snap on a pair of latex gloves. He opened the kit and attached the needle. Not putting the syringe down, he tore open an alcohol swab and cleaned the top of the ampule, then punctured the seal and drew out the clear fluid. He pointed the needle toward the ceiling and tapped out an air bubble. For a split second, the tip caught the light just right and was the brightest object in the room. He turned toward the array of IV pumps and tubes.

"What's your pain level," he asked, while he opened a second alcohol wipe and sterilized the injection port.

With my right hand I flashed five and three. His eyebrows shot up; his jaw tightened.

I watched closely as the needle pierced the membrane, almost flesh-colored.

He frowned, concentrating on his task. "Well, help is on the way," he said, carefully squeezing the syringe.

Daniel was one of my best nurses. He was among the most conscientious, and was friendly and upbeat. He was closer to my age than most of the professional staff, and we had some common interests. He was also one of my wife's and daughter's favorites. He was one of the "regulars," and I considered myself lucky I got his help frequently, usually for three or four days in a row, about two weeks each month. He was of medium height and build, with wavy light brown hair that was graying at the closely-trimmed sides. A well-tended soul patch below his lower lip hinted of his previous career as a professional musician.

I watched the syringe empty into the IV, the transparent liquids mingling, moving down the line and through the insertion site into my bruised and bony arm. I pictured the tiny molecules of Dilaudid pulsing through my vein, moving toward my heart.

Daniel stepped away to dispose of the sharp and gloves. He turned back with a kind look and a resolute half-smile.

"Get some rest, Geo."

He left, closing the door behind him. I was grateful to him; I thought what a great guy he was. I felt bad that I lied to him – but the regret only lasted a moment, as the feeling I sought began flooding my body.

I was lying because I wasn't in such distress when I called for a shot. I was probably at only two or three on the pain scale, not eight. In reality, I didn't have a lot of the worst pain anymore. I no longer suffered the constant and often overwhelming full-body clench or cramp. In those earlier days, I couldn't sleep or even rest without the pain shots. Over time and with therapy loosening me up, the need had faded. But another need had taken its place.

The almost immediate mental and physical rush of an IV narcotic injection is a seductive, potentially addicting sensation. After four months and longer of up to twelve shots a day, I was clearly addicted. Yet I denied that this sensation was my compulsion. In my rationalization, the new purpose of the pain shots was to allow me to briefly escape being fully conscious of this nightmare existence. Softening the impact of my condition and surroundings on my psyche was therapeutic, I decided.

But now those escapes weren't coming as often as they had. Not long before this injection, Dr. Kumar cut the frequency from every two hours to every four. And they were to be given at my request, not on a set schedule. It was understood I would ask for only as much as needed and eventually taper off on my own.

That restriction irritated me; I didn't want to wait that long between shots. For quite some time I was becoming anxious for the next shot well before the two-hour mark, and lately had noticed the buzz didn't last as long, and was gradually getting shorter. Waiting for four hours was so upsetting, I had no intention of weaning myself off the narcotics at this point, or considering it any time soon. And since I couldn't move myself, it didn't matter if I was drugged up and sluggish in therapy. I saw no benefit in quitting.

In addition, I felt entitled to it. This was payback for my suffering; it was my only fun, a well-deserved distraction from my dismal existence. I was owed these happy moments when I could lay back and enjoy how good my body felt when the rush hit, and how I didn't have to pay attention for a while. I earned the right to turn down the volume and dim the lights.

I thought the drugs were doing no harm.

With Daniel gone and the door closed, my guilt about lying was quickly blotted out as the Dilaudid took effect. The rush came on strong; in that moment it was my only friend, the only thing I cared about. I felt relief to get my next dose and, strangely, the satisfaction of having accomplished something. The rush was emotional, not just physical.

It started with heat in my chest that spread out to my limbs. It was like my bones were radiator pipes warming my body from the inside, while on the outside, hundreds of balls of soft, fuzzy cotton pushed in on me. I felt my skin itching – and bliss.

I lay there, and random thoughts swirled in my brain like so many specks of dust dancing in a beam of sunlight. The drug wrapped me in a warm cocoon of forgetfulness, and I stared at the wall where nothing ever changed, not even the clock.

I awoke deep in the night. The call button was not under my hand. The old anxiety shot through me: I was cut off from help.

It was safely under my right hand when I fell asleep but now was next to my forearm just below the elbow. It seemed impossible I missed someone coming in, lifting my hand, and moving it while I remained undisturbed. Nothing else in the room had changed. But someone had come in while I was unconscious, and they placed the call button aside for a moment and forgot to put it back.

My heart was racing with worry while I stared at it. I wanted it badly. The call button wasn't just close, it was touching my arm. It was torturous to be in physical contact with something I needed for survival but couldn't reach to use, because I couldn't lift my arm to pick it up.

I noticed the cord was still in its place, running lengthwise from the top of the bed down toward my hand, making a U-turn a few inches above my wrist. I had an idea: *Can I get it with my other hand?*

Laurie had me doing exercises called "spider crawling" the last few weeks, where you pull your hand along with your fingers. This was farther to go than any previous effort, but it was my only chance. I had to try. *Let's see if this works.*

Concentrating hard, I curled my left thumb as much as I could while pressing down on the sheet. The hand moved half an inch. *At least it moved.* I did it again and again, moving only a fraction of an inch each time. After dozens of moves, I brought my arm up to a ninety-degree angle across my belly. I felt the shape of the G-J tube connector under my fingers and the weight of my hand on the site.

Okay. On to phase two. Now I needed to move the hand across my body to beyond the other arm. I curled my gnarled fingers and saw it move a little. *So far so good.* I kept at it, with each curling of my fingers pulling the hand closer to the loop of cord. Time stopped for me as the hand creeped along until I made it to the arm. In two more moves I was able to stretch out my finger and hook the cord at its U-turn.

Now control it. I pushed down to straighten my arm and the cord, to pull the button down to where I could slide my right hand over it. I don't think I blinked once while I slowly brought it down. Finally, I slipped my hand over the device, clutching it possessively. *That's it. That's it!*

I was tired and relieved, and, despite the mood meds, mildly excited. I realized this event was different from other "firsts" in my recovery. This was the first time since getting sick I was able to act on or manipulate something outside my own body. In addition, it was the first time I pushed myself and did something I didn't know I could do. I recognized this was some kind of breakthrough.

$\mathbf{A}$bout ten in the morning on the first Friday of September, I was greeted by Marielle's melodic voice when she and her assistant, Deborah, came into the room rolling a contraption that looked like a tall desk with a laminate top.

"Good morning, Mr. Walsh!" she called. She turned toward me, clasped her hands together, and grinned. Apparently, she had an announcement.

"Okay! Today," she paused, drawing out my suspense, "we're going to get you up on your feet." My eyes popped open in surprise. "This is a standing frame and it will support you. We've got to do this to get you standing, and we need to get you standing so you can start walking!"

I didn't believe her. I thought she was humoring me. *How can I ever walk again?*

Marielle and Deborah locked the frame's wheels, adjusted its height, and made sure my tubes were out of the way. Then they swung my legs out and brought my shoulders up in one fluid motion.

They grasped my upper arms and stood me up. For the first time since I climbed onto the gurney in the ER more than five months ago, my feet felt a hard surface beneath them. Marielle asked me to step toward the frame, but I only shuffled as they moved me. I noticed my feet were somewhat curled up, especially my left, which was also turned inward a little. That leg felt odd; it seemed it was shorter than the other or not solid on the ground. I felt the floor, but the leg lacked sensation deep inside all the way to my hip. It felt hollow. I wondered what that meant.

I leaned over the frame on my elbows. Marielle held me steady while Deborah brought a wide woven strap behind my legs just under my bottom and attached it to the other side. Then she cinched it tight, which pulled my hips up over my knees, straightening my legs. I was forced to stand, propped up like a figurine mounted for exhibition.

Within moments my knees started to hurt. They hadn't been straightened or felt any weight on them in months. Then the tendons and the leg bones themselves began to ache, and then my hips. I pushed down on my forearms to take some weight off, but I was too weak to make any difference. I began to sweat as the pain rose into my lower back.

I looked over at Marielle. She was watching me like a mother hawk; her soft brown eyes were alert while her smile radiated encouragement. I knew she wanted me to do well, but also that she'd let me quit and lie back down as soon as I wanted. That was so tempting. The strain became more intense. I turned away and slumped over.

Marielle knew I was faltering but wasn't ready to let me give up.

"Head up!" she sang out.

I lifted my chin and looked out the window. The blinds were

all the way up, and I could see much more of the nurses' station than when I sat on the bed. I was glad, hoping the new view would distract me and help me stay up longer before I couldn't take it anymore. I understood bearing the pain was my job today.

Then it struck me: it wasn't just today. This was only the beginning.

With this new stage of therapy, the responsibility for my recovery had shifted to me. The hard work had begun, work that could make me independent – work only I could do. I also had the sudden awareness that in the back of my mind I had been waiting for this moment since the night I came to this hospital.

My thoughts went back to that evening, and I recalled what Dr. Nguyen and the transport driver said to me, what they called me. And now I had come to the part of the journey where I could prove their words were true. I knew it would be the hardest job I ever had, but – at least inside my own skin, within the personal arena of one insignificant individual's rehabilitation – I still had a chance to be a "great man."

I looked back at Marielle. *Maybe she's right, and I will walk again,* I thought.

Her eyes seemed to be cheering me on. I felt a pang of desire to make her proud, and to be proud of myself.

I want them all to be proud of me.

The explosion of brilliant colors floating in the middle of the room was a vivid contrast to my washed-out surroundings. I stared up in a happy daze at the bunch of big, shiny balloons my wife brought for me – happy because of the sentiment, dazed by the iridescent material and the bright saturated hues of festive cartoon images like cupcakes, presents, party hats, and candles. There were not as many candles as I needed, though. It was my sixtieth birthday.

I wasn't cutting the cake or popping the cork. I wasn't being toasted by family, friends, and neighbors. I got pain shots instead.

It didn't matter if I wasn't up for a party; I just appreciated how remarkable it was that I was still here. I looked back over everything that happened to me in the past year, and found it hard to believe. But those were my memories, and I was still stuck in this bed, so I had to accept it was all real.

One year ago, I thought my life had no value, I didn't deserve it, and I'd be helping my family by taking it. On this birthday, all I wanted was to be alive.

"The effects of the toxin can last up to six months," Dr. Kumar said to my wife on one of the first days I was under his care. Totally locked-in and desperate for good news, I decided this meant I'd be home and generally healthy by then. I imagined the toxin had temporarily blocked, not destroyed, my nerves' ability to function, and in six months I'd be back to where I was on that warm spring morning before the storm.

While riding the rapids of the daily routine and navigating through pain, physical challenges, equipment malfunction, and human error, I usually didn't think about the status of my overall progress. The unceasing activity, cocktail of anti-depressive drugs, and the staff's encouragement kept me in the moment and my head down, focused on my work. But when reaching a landmark such as the six-month anniversary of getting sick, I was confronted with the big picture.

I awoke very early that morning, well aware of the date. I started measuring how much I'd improved, but it struck me more forcefully how little had changed. There was such a wide chasm between where I expected to be and where I was that I scolded myself for my foolish magical thinking. This negativity toward myself magnified my disappointment at the lack of progress.

After six harrowing months, there were so many basic things

I still could not do. Breathe on my own, nourish myself, speak without the PMV. Touch my face, operate the bed controls. Move off the bed or stand without maximum assistance. Roll over in bed so I could turn away from the never-changing view of cabinets, sink, clock, sharps box, television, computer.

I felt overwhelmed by the unfairness of my situation, my frustration at being useless, and the pointlessness of struggling so hard for a greatly diminished future. Because, I thought, a circumscribed future is what my lack of progress foretold. If the toxin is gone or nearly gone and I'm still in such terrible condition, what hope do I have of returning to a normal life?

I looked blankly across the room at the beams of early morning sunlight slanting across the wall of white cabinets as I felt myself falling into despair.

I understood what was happening to me; I experienced these down moods before. I had the presence of mind to know I should meet these emotions head-on, and I must fight back. I sensed I needed a weapon that was the exact opposite of this engulfing feeling of being cheated, of being the victim of an injustice. And it occurred to me the opposite of feeling robbed is feeling grateful. Despite the hopelessness flooding my heart, I knew it was true. I needed to be thankful. But, for what?

As my mind reached for that something, I gazed at those golden-orange rays falling on the cabinets. Through my dry, crusted-over eyes I stared at the angled amber shapes and marveled that this illumination came from millions of miles away. I noted it was only in recent weeks these beams of early light had become visible on the wall, and they were moving farther into the room and higher on the wall each morning, tracking the movement of the sun as it rose later and farther to the south at this time of the year, which itself was only one phase of the majestic annual cycle of the seasons.

Then I realized, although the morning sun was now in a position where I could see its light, its light had always been coming into my room, every day I've been here.

I had not seen the sun nor felt its warmth for a full six months, yet it was always up there. I could not see it now, but in front of me I could see evidence of the sun. I was witness to its light and power, and by its brilliance and changing position I could measure the passage of time as the world turned beneath me and life went on around me.

This all went through my mind in a flash, and then words came to me, unscripted, unsought, and my lips moved silently at the same instant the words formed in my head.

Thank you, God, for bringing me one day closer to getting out of here.

I don't know where it came from; I hadn't been thinking about God or spirituality. At least not consciously. I suppose somewhere inside me I knew it was the right thing to do. It was; this spontaneous, silent prayer was answered by a reversal in my thinking. This simple expression of thanks made me feel thankful, by reminding me I had much to be grateful for. And in thanking God I included all that had happened to me and everything I was a part of – the near miracle of the first doctor saving my life, the love and support of my family, the care and compassion of Dr. Kumar, the awesome infrastructure of medical knowledge and technology in which I was enmeshed – in sum, the life force carrying me along.

With gratitude also came an acceptance of and resignation to my situation. With this clarity, my fragile resolve began to rebuild.

But there was a second part of my prayer: the acknowledgment that someday I'd get out of here. Somehow, just as expressing gratitude inspired gratitude, by asserting I would get out of here one day, that day became real.

It had been an abstract concept, if I let myself think of it at all. I was existing day-to-day. Now, my mind accepted that this phase of my illness, my time in this hospital, would someday come to an end. As I came to that understanding, I noticed an odd tingling, and realized it was an experience I hadn't felt for a long time: the physical sensation of anticipation. Just as in normal life you might think about your dinner plans tomorrow or an appointment next week, I could feel the certainty of and a connection with a particular day in my future: *that day*.

Outside my door I heard the sounds of the next shift arriving at the nurses' station, the prelude to the rush and routine that would soon wash over me. I lay there and watched those beams of morning light change from amber to white while they slowly moved down the cabinets and out of sight until tomorrow.

Another day had begun, one day closer to *that day*.

Sometimes, when I tried to recall the care, treatments, or occurrences of the day before – or even that morning – I was like a man on an ocean voyage trying to remember a particular wave he passed. Everything would blur together, and on a journey confined to this cheerless room, I often felt I was going nowhere. I knew I would get out of the hospital someday but feared it could be years. I compared my confinement with a convict's and decided I had it worse: if I had been sentenced to prison at least I'd know when they must release me, but here I was serving an indefinite sentence.

Yet, day by day, progress was being made. Speech therapy was going well, as my neck and throat muscles continued to regain movement faster than the rest of my body. I got the high-tech therapeutic bed and gained some lung capacity, which gave me more strength and energy for other therapies. I was sitting up on the side of the bed and in a wheelchair. For short periods I was able to tolerate being off the ventilator, using oxygen, breathing on my own.

Occupational therapy was bringing improvements as Laurie pushed me full speed ahead. I learned she was a fitness fanatic, which I had guessed, and would often mention her group workouts in different routines she tried. She complained how hot she became with her long, thick, curly hair, but sought out the most challenging classes. A true go-getter, she was part of a real go-getter family, with a husband in a professional field and teens excelling in sports, academics, and music. I felt lucky to be one of her projects.

"This is going to hurt until it doesn't," she was saying one afternoon while pulling my left elbow away from my side and massaging my shoulder blade. The rub felt good but there were sharp pains in the joint itself.

"You've made a lot of progress, though. You only had, well, almost no range of motion when we first started working together. Now you're up to about sixty degrees."

She nodded with an appraising look. "Good job, Geo," she said, not stopping the exercise. I smiled at her encouragement and the underserved compliment.

With her help, some of my finer motor skills were returning, but it looked like I'd never make a fist or have a normal grip. My ring and little fingers on both hands were curled in and twisted, looking a bit like corkscrews. Some osteoarthritis must have set in during the early days of my botulism, probably triggered by stress and overall inflammation. This was disturbing. I wondered if I could ever use a knife and fork again, or if I'll be able to type. Playing piano or picking up a guitar seemed just a sad memory.

I had been able to put my hands on my belly for a while, and as my arm strength grew, I began to reach farther up my body. I passed the G-J tube site and felt the fat ridged ventilator hoses. Before long, I passed the ventilator hoses and touched the square connector box. Eventually I made my way to the narrow single air tube and then to the tracheostomy itself. It was disconcerting to feel a plastic pipe jutting from the base of my neck and, when I pressed against it, its movement inside my throat.

A few days later I reached my chin and felt my new goatee. That was a strange sensation: I never grew a beard before. In another week, I touched the tip of my nose – and was able to scratch it for the first time in seven months.

Just past mid-October, my wife decided my hands had improved enough to hold a mirror and take a look at myself.

"Well, you can't hold it, but it ought to stay up . . . there you go," she said, nestling the handle inside my loose grip. The mirror tipped but stabilized. I could see the wall behind me; I twisted my hand to shift the angle and there was my face. It showed no reaction.

"That's you now, honey. What do you think?"

Part of me was shocked, the shock of recognition – I could still see me. The greater part of me was clinical. I wanted to memorize in detail how I appeared to the world, see what everyone else saw.

It was a sobering sight. The shape of my skull exposed under the tight, desiccated skin. Wisps of colorless hair over a shiny scalp. Deep hollows at my temples and under sharp cheek bones. The slash of a mouth set within a bush of white whiskers. A beak-like nose jutting from the flushed face. Haunted, burning eyes staring at me from cavernous depths.

Others may find in such a moment cause for regret, but I was analytical. I concluded I was an old man now, and life had passed me by. Yet, as I stared into my gleaming, sunken eyes, I felt a kind of defiance, perhaps pride, well up inside me. I acknowledged to myself with no small measure of satisfaction, *You're still here, man.*

My increasing dexterity allowed me to hold a mirror and see myself again, but in it Laurie saw a sign I was ready for a better way to communicate. One afternoon she brought in a fat felt-tip marker, wrapped in gauze and tape to make it easier for me to grip. She put it in my hand and a steno pad on my lap.

I could barely hold the marker tip to the paper, and my hand shook while I made the first line of the first letter of my simple message: "Hello." It was ridiculous how wobbly my initial attempt to write again was. Within a few days, however, the hand steadied, and since I could communicate more complex thoughts so much easier on paper, our amazing alphabet system at which I had become so skilled was abandoned and never used again.

Halloween, mid-morning, Marielle and Deborah appeared outside my door moving a piece of equipment I hadn't seen before. They stopped when I could see half of what looked like a standing frame, except with bigger wheels and a thick blue top. Marielle came in the room and Deborah followed with a wheelchair.

"Good morning, Mister Walsh," Marielle said, drawing out her words. Once again, she had an announcement, and that meant more work for me. With new equipment involved I knew it would be hard, and it might hurt. I began to feel nervous.

Marielle took a deep breath and clasped her hands in front of her. She started slowly but ended in a rush of words.

"Today . . . is the day . . . we get you up and walking!" She beamed at me.

I tilted my head and gave her a skeptical look. Even though my legs were getting stronger from the standing frame and some light exercises in bed, this seemed too soon. But if they thought I was ready, I was ready to try. As "Mountain Man" once told me, I had to start sometime.

I was motivated but had one regret, and it was a big one: my wife wasn't there. She deserved to see this. She usually came before this time of day, but for some reason – bad traffic, an errand perhaps – she hadn't arrived.

"Okay, someone already put your shoes on, so let's get you up," Marielle said. Her voice was calm and steady while they worked. "Lower the rail . . . we've got the Foley, Deborah? The nurse disconnected your IV and feeding . . . wheelchair locked . . . take you off room oxygen." She lifted the cannula over my head and away from the tracheostomy. For the first time since intubation, I had no breathing support.

"Now . . . on your side . . . legs over . . . and bring you up," Marielle narrated as she and Deborah sat me on the edge of the bed. I was a little afraid and tried to focus my thoughts. *I've got to try hard.*

They each took an arm and stood me up. Even aided, doing my little quarter-turn shuffle without oxygen was a strain. They let me down into the wheelchair, and Marielle resumed the O2 support from a tank behind the seat. Then Deborah rolled me out the door and up to the walking frame. It had much larger wheels than the standing frame, no belt to secure me, a padded horseshoe-shaped top to lean on, and a pair of handles I could grab.

"We'll hold you up while you're walking," Marielle said, "and bring the wheelchair right behind you. If you get tired, just sit down. Just plop down. We've got you. Now, we'll bring you up, and you reach for the handles."

The ladies stood me up within the horseshoe, and I took hold of the handles. My grip was weak, as only my thumb and first two fingers worked, like a pincer. I still had the hollow feeling in my left leg.

I was now in position, the wheels were unlocked, and Marielle said, "Okay, step out with your right foot. Step."

I was shocked by my weakness and lack of coordination when I took my first steps. I just kicked my foot forward less than a shoe's length, with it hardly leaving the ground. Then the left leg jerked far forward and landed almost in front of the right.

"Right to the right, left to the left," Deborah called in a monotone.

Surprised by my lack of control, staring down, I gathered my concentration to take my third step. Then, just as I kicked out my right foot again, in my peripheral vision I saw my wife coming down the hallway from the elevators.

Much more than for my sake, I was happy for her that she would witness this. It was her advocacy and dedication that had brought me to this milestone. But I could not acknowledge her; I was keeping my head down, focused on the floor in front of me and my feet below.

So I didn't see her pull out her phone and capture the next fifty-eight seconds on video.

In it, I see myself approaching, an emaciated figure in a yellow gown hanging to above my knees, hunched over the frame's blue-cushioned top. My hands are like claws; my arms nothing but bone and sinew, a detached IV connector dangling off the near one, both bruised in several places. The legs are thin as sticks of balsa wood with no apparent muscle; my left foot turning in, my gait a lurching clip-clop. On each side, the two women in dark blue scrubs move along with me, keeping me upright, pulling the wheelchair behind. Marielle is on the closer side, her long ponytail swaying with each step.

I come up to the camera, and my head looms larger in the frame. The stark overhead lighting reveals the skeletal profile, sunken cheeks, head turned down, face focused but showing no emotion, eyes staring out beyond the handgrips.

Just as I pass, still moving forward, my chin jerks up and I look out ahead of me. Even with the video's volume off, every time I watch this moment, I hear Marielle call out.

"Head up!"

I don't remember how far I went that day, perhaps fifty feet. Once my energy was gone, I was taken back in the wheelchair and transferred to the bed. I did not complete the round-trip, but Marielle was very pleased.

"Mr. Walsh, that was a good start! You went farther than I thought," she said happily. Her smile was encouraging and kind. "Good for you."

My wife was happy too, but I don't know what she said once we were alone. I fell asleep in minutes. I was exhausted and not at all excited. I saw this as just the first rung on a new, higher, and steeper ladder I had to climb. It was just another day on the job where the job keeps getting harder. Although it was the first time I was upright and moving forward under my own power in over seven months, in my mind that was but a waypoint on the journey, a mark on the map now behind me.

Another steep increase in monthly health insurance premiums forced me out of the PPO plan that let me see my rock-star surgeon, but we didn't save money. For the same price, as of the first of November I was enrolled in the inferior HMO plan selected by my wonderful former employer. The last HMO denied care and medications for my Crohn's, which brought about a life-threatening crisis, so I was naturally concerned this HMO would cause problems. But my hospitalization, ventilator, medicines, and therapy were all unquestionably a "medical necessity," their usual complaint. My care had been going on for months and would need to continue for many more. I thought, *What can they do to me?*

My wife stormed in one afternoon around mid-month, closing the door hard. Her face wore a look of anger mixed with fear. I never saw her like this before. I was worried. Something was wrong. She clutched some papers in her hand.

"Big problem. Those – uhh!" She pounded her palm into the arm of the chair. After taking a breath to compose herself she continued through gritted teeth.

"I just talked to Linda downstairs in case management, and she says that the HMO says that since you got sick while on the PPO plan, the PPO is responsible for all your care related to this disease until you're better. But the PPO says no, you are off their plan as of the first, so any costs from that day forward are the responsibility of the HMO." She was becoming more agitated.

"Since the PPO says you're not their patient, and the HMO says you're not their patient, Linda says you've had no health insurance since the start of the month. That means it's all on us. It's all our responsibility." Her eyes darted around the room and began filling with tears. "Oh, Geo, this is going to ruin us!"

My eyes popped open and my palms shot out. I didn't expect any big changes, but this was as big as it gets. The HMO was throwing me into the street.

I was astonished. I felt threatened. I was in the hands of a faceless, soulless "health management organization" that would ration my care by denying all care. This was corporate cost-saving excuse-making taken to a previously unheard-of level of evil.

I wondered if the county hospital would take me. My care wouldn't even be as good as this place, but I supposed I'd survive. I heard they didn't provide any therapy.

My wife looked at me. Her eyes narrowed; I saw her determination. "I'm sure this is all bullshit to try to wiggle out of their responsibility for the cost for this. Linda said nobody ever tried this trick before and thinks it can't be legal. They have to cave. So, I'm going to get on them, and Dr. Kumar is going to call and get on them."

She slapped the arm of the chair again and rolled her eyes. "Oh, and get this. Linda says I have to call someone named Kaitlin at your old office for some kind of continuous coverage form she was supposed to mail to us – last month!" I was thankful I had an advocate at that moment. In my condition there was no way I could deal with any of this, and they'd simply ship me out.

There I was, still deep in long-term acute care, racking up charges for the room, the ventilator, doctors, nursing care, equipment fees, and medicines amounting to thousands of dollars every single day, and the HMO was trying to wash their hands of me.

No matter how this was going to turn out, by their ruthless behavior I knew the HMO was laying down a marker: they wanted me out of there – stat.

Part Five

As autumn advanced, daylight came later and the room darkened early. I was living more and more under the pulsating glow of fluorescent bulbs, which cast a cold pallor on the blurred, unvarying scene. Although the backdrop was only slowly shifting, this seasonal change pressed upon me an awareness of the long passage of time since I arrived here.

The fluorescents in the room included the ceiling lights but also a smaller light over the head of the bed for the patient to control. Someone added a length to the cord so it could lay near my hands, but try as I might I could not switch the light on or off. It illustrates the depth of my incapacitation that in my eighth month of hospitalization, I was still too weak to pull a light cord using both arms.

In the later part of November, while we were fighting with the HMO – Linda was right, they finally had to admit I was their patient – improvement quickened on many fronts.

Speech was doing well as far as articulation goes, but I was not doing well at reaching one of our main goals, passing the swallow test. I had to get past this before I could eat, and I already flunked three.

In occupational therapy, my shoulders were mobile enough that Laurie had me start weightlifting in bed. We began with a one-pound bar, the lightest one in the set. It was humbling that a guy who used to scoop up two toddlers on the run and hoist them to his shoulders now struggled to lift one pound.

She also taught me to coordinate my breathing with each lift, and to break the session into reps and sets. Learning these techniques enabled me to do much more work than I expected, and I knew they would be useful when I'm out on my own.

Physical therapy was walking. Progress was measured in going farther overall or making fewer stops. Marielle and her assistant handled most of these sessions, and while Deborah chanted, "Left to the left, right to the right," Marielle would make sure I kept my "Head up!" But almost every time I set a new distance record I was working with Kate.

Dr. Kumar was frustrated with my slow progress weaning off the vent. The high-tech bed and continued therapy, including the PMV, made significant improvements, but the increase in capacity had hit a plateau. Nevertheless, I began sitting up in a wheelchair, on oxygen, off the vent.

In this situation, with the cuff deflated and the trach plugged, breathing in the normal fashion through my nose and mouth, I was able to talk again. After eight months of silence except for the few hours each week with the PMV, I could just talk.

Many of the regular staff who were used to me being the stone-faced patient were startled when I first spoke to them. But it was a good surprise. I was grateful to be able to say "Good morning" again and "Thank you." That was very important to me. I always tried to make eye contact and smile so they knew it came from the bottom of my heart.

It was strange to feel the vibrations in my throat and hear my voice again. It wasn't really my voice, though, the one I remembered. It came in short bursts of breath with a quavering tone, hesitant pace, higher pitch, a definite slur. To me it sounded like the voice of a very old man. It pained me to think of myself that way.

One of the greatest benefits of speaking was I could help manage my own care. This let my wife and daughter skip some visits. At first it was only on weekends, as we knew the hospital didn't admit patients then, and I'd be safe from being moved to a double room. I was happy they could start getting back to their own lives and enjoying themselves a little.

One of the first things my wife did with this freedom was join a meetup group with her sister-in-law, and every Friday they'd hike up a local trail and share wine and cheese on the summit at sunset. I was amazed – to relax from her long and stressful week she went and pushed herself even farther. It seemed she always had another mountain to climb.

I was talking to Dr. Kumar about my swallow test scheduled for that afternoon.

"If I pass this one, if four's the charm, can I get something to eat this evening? Yogurt, or at least some ice chips to start?"

Dr. Kumar frowned. "The swallow test is not the final step before eating," he said. "You will still have to pass an intestinal motility X-ray before I can let you eat. Swallowing is one thing, but you have to be able to pass the food through the intestine as well. I'm sorry."

"I didn't know that," I said, dismayed. "How soon can we get that done?"

The doctor shook his head. "At least one week after you pass the swallow test."

This hit me like a blow. No one told me about this second test before. I had been looking forward to today's exam, I thought I would pass, but now I didn't care how well I did.

When Rachel came in later, I was lethargic while she was energized. Passing the swallow test wasn't just my goal, my success would also reflect on her. Getting a tough case like me over the finish line would be quite an accomplishment.

She gave me tips on how to swallow: slow, deliberate, forceful. She told me this before, and I was sure I could get it right. Rachel was confident too. Outside the X-ray lab she gave me a final pep talk.

"Now just remember what I said. One strong motion. It will look good on the X-ray."

I did pass. I was pleased, but knowing I still couldn't eat put a damper on my happiness. In contrast to my lack of enthusiasm, Rachel was thrilled. And she had an idea how to celebrate. As soon as we were outside the X-ray department, she told me her plan.

"Hey, Geo, y'know what? I want to kind of surprise everybody back at the nurses' station when we go back up? So, when we come off the elevator, I want you to be like, all dejected, like you didn't pass again. And then when we get up to the station and they ask how it went, I'll be like, 'Well . . . ' Kind of sad? And then go, 'He passed!'" she sang out in a muted voice. "Then I'll go into my happy dance!"

Grinning, she shimmied her shoulders to rehearse her routine. I looked skeptical and didn't say anything. I was thinking about food.

Still smiling, she lifted her eyebrows and asked, "Are you game?"

I smiled back. "Okay. I'll do it."

"Alright! Let's go!" She turned the wheelchair and headed for the elevator.

When we exited on the third floor, I played my part. I hung my head and frowned, avoiding eye contact. I shook my head once or twice, looking rueful, I thought. I couldn't see Rachel's expression but heard the disappointment in her voice when we reached the station.

"I'm bringing Mr. Walsh back from his swallow test," she said flatly.

No one spoke at first. Our act convinced everyone I failed again, and being professionals, they weren't going to react in a negative way and amplify my sad feelings. In a bland tone, not glancing up from his paperwork, one nurse mumbled, "And how'd that go?"

"Well," Rachel began, and let out a dramatic sigh. "He . . ." she paused again, then cried out, "He passed! Whoo-hoo! Happy dance!"

I twisted around to see her celebrating our success, then turned back at the staff in surprise – they were clapping, a few cheered, and many congratulated me. The wave of joy Rachel started washed over me. Her enthusiasm, and a little bit of showmanship, made me appreciate what a big step this was.

Beginning in the last week of November, I was allowed and able to breathe on my own for short periods. I would sit in the wheelchair, off the vent, with no oxygen, the cuff deflated, for almost an hour. The staff called it "being on room air." I don't remember the first time I could do it; I'm sure I didn't get excited. Even that milestone was just one of many moments of gradual, continual improvement.

This gave me a new freedom, though we didn't realize it until Dr. Kumar brought it up with my wife and me late morning on the first of December.

"Mrs. Walsh, George is doing so well now, there is no need for him to stay here in the room. Perhaps, if you care to take him, he would enjoy going outside."

"That's a great idea. What do you think, sweetie?"

"Outside? Outside . . . the building?" The idea bothered me. I knew I should be happy for the opportunity but didn't want to go.

"Of course, outside," my wife said. Turning to the doctor, she asked, "You do mean outside the building, don't you?"

"Yes." He chuckled and waved his arm. "Outside the building."

"That will be great! We'll do it," my wife exclaimed.

You'd think I'd be eager to get out of my little bubble, but I felt annoyed; I felt as if I were being pitied. I didn't want a break, thank you very much. My mind was tightly compartmentalized; I knew the contents and the shape of my miniature world and could cope within its limits. I didn't want to open that box and peek out at "the real world," and be reminded of what I was missing.

"Yeah. Great," I said softly.

A nurse came with a wheelchair and bundled me up with blankets across my legs and narrow shoulders. In a few minutes we came out into the corridor. All eyes at the nurses' station were on me; they were excited for me. I knew I too should be excited, but couldn't enjoy the moment.

We got on the elevator with a younger couple wearing visitor's wristbands. I saw the man earlier, during my PT, when he was chatting with several nurses and staffers at the station. I presumed he was a former patient who came back to show off how well he's doing and felt happy for him. Seeing him again on the elevator, I wondered if he and I had something in common.

For months, different staffers told me, "You're in the lucky room." My room had a reputation for good outcomes on tough cases, they said. They mentioned a case from the previous year as proof. It was a younger man who had Guillain-Barré, who was paralyzed from the neck down and on a ventilator for over six months. Now, they heard, he's surfing again. Could this fellow in the elevator be that man?

I looked up at the couple. Their eyes were locked. His face was lit with a beaming smile; in hers I saw affection and relief.

I thought of asking him if he had been in "the lucky room," but couldn't bring myself to intrude on their privacy. I didn't want to draft him into an obligation to lift my spirits, or drag him back into this world from which he escaped, where we're all flying before the storm and fighting to keep up hope. I looked away; it was encouragement enough to see their faces.

We came off the elevator and down a long hallway toward the bright glow of the lobby ahead. The first floor was much larger than the upper stories. I was confused by the many doors and hallways, paintings and posters, people coming and going and walking by. The lobby dazzled me with its glass walls and high ceiling, dark leather couches, polished stone floor, and sweeping granite reception desk. My eyes darted from detail to detail. Then, outside the windows I saw a planter full of flowers, some trees, a parking lot, other buildings farther away. I was stunned.

The two sets of automatic doors swooshed open. I felt the increased humidity, the moist air bathing my papery skin and parched eyes. From under the covered portico we turned onto a smaller path to an octagonal patio surrounded by a wide, lush lawn.

It had rained over the weekend, leaving the sky a uniform leaden gray. The surrounding trees and bushes were dark misshapen smudges, but the lawn glowed a deep emerald.

With the dim, diffused lighting there were no shadows, just a vague darkness on the undersides of the bushes and trees. Seen through my unfocusing eyes, this created a strange visual effect: with no shadows and no angle of the sun, there was no depth or dimension to the scene nor a sense it was any particular time of day. Everything looked familiar yet fake, as if I were on a stage surrounded by a painted backdrop.

In an instant the illusion was shattered by something undeniably real: the devastating, sweet, vibrant smell of the lawn around us. Its elemental aroma of earth, water, and living grass penetrated deep into my mind – so fresh and clean, so alive.

My sense of smell had been dulled by the disease, perhaps by the same process that caused my dry mouth and eyes. I never noticed any offensive hospital odors or smelled my wife's take-out dinners. But now, in a split second, the sensation returned, pure and intense. I shuddered at the impact. It was intoxicating. It was strong medicine, and it was hard to take.

I inhaled long breaths through my nose, exhaling more slowly through my mouth, as they taught me. The rich, delicious scent filled my entire head – I felt it at the back of my neck – but it also stirred up thoughts I didn't want to face. Condensed in that smell were hundreds of memories, all involving grass – running down a hill, feeling its crunch under bare feet, laying on it, mowing it, baseball games, backyards, barbecues.

I had been blocking out thoughts about such precious things, and my emotions were in turmoil. I knew I should enjoy the fresh air and happy memories but it was exhausting. Although I wanted to be a good patient and stay longer, I gave up.

"Okay, I want to go back up now," I blurted.

"But, honey, it's only been like, fifteen minutes," my wife replied. She gave me a questioning look. "It's been so long since you've been outside."

I was impatient. "It's too much. It's enough," I snapped back. From the look on her face I knew that didn't make sense. *I don't want to sound ungrateful. What excuse would a normal person understand?* I softened my tone. "I'm getting cold now. Please take me back up."

"Oh, alright." She smiled and stepped behind me. She rubbed my bony shoulder. "You don't have much insulation on you, do you?"

"Nope. Not no more," I joked, trying to hide my feelings.

As we turned toward the hospital, I glanced up at the third-floor windows and wondered: *Which one is my room, the lucky room?*

The chair rocked and rattled over the weathered pavement as we approached the lobby entrance. I recalled the last time I was outdoors, more than seven months earlier, when I was brought to this hospital. That evening, I was helpless, strapped to a gurney, totally locked-in, terrified by the mere sound of the wind and its movement across my face.

On this morning, the world seemed much more benign. I just wasn't ready to go back there yet.

Every day, three times a day, aides pushed their lumbering carts laden with covered food trays down the hall and never stopped outside my door. That didn't bother me early in my paralysis, because I didn't experience hunger. In time, however, the psychological craving to enjoy different tastes and textures began to trouble me. It grew more intense as the months wore on.

I told everyone I couldn't wait to eat the fettuccine Alfredo at our favorite restaurant again. A nurse supervisor promised to buy me a burger and beer when I was out; I could not imagine eating something as large as a hamburger again. One of my CNA buddies would tease me, asking things like, "If you could have your choice, right now, would you prefer a porterhouse, New York or rib-eye steak? Have you ever tasted wagyu beef?"

I knew I couldn't have steak for my first meal, but I did not expect the horror I was given to eat for the intestinal motility test – a practically flavorless, dry, rubbery, institutional-quality egg salad on white bread sandwich, laced with an imaging contrast chemical. And since I was technically still NPO, I couldn't have even a sip of water to help me swallow. I was only able to choke down half of the awful thing while the tech recorded how well it moved through me.

The first three images showed I wasn't going to pass, but we completed the series over its several hours anyway. It was a difficult and disappointing day. The test revealed intermittent motility but nothing like normal peristalsis. It was not yet safe for me to eat.

I was getting impatient for my favorite foods, but I'd have to wait a while longer.

Dr. Barone always greeted every patient the same way, with a cascade of words in a droning, descending melody. My door was open that morning, and I heard several personalized versions of it as he stopped at other patients' room on his way to mine.

"Good morning, Mr. Walsh, how's it going?" He walked in making a quick half wave. He was a slight man with sprinkles of gray in his dark hair, talkative about the medicine but otherwise shy. He pushed his dark-framed glasses up his nose, then his hand stayed loose in the air, gesturing while he spoke.

"Well, I've been looking at your case and your projected timetable, and I think we can start planning ahead on where you go for rehab when you're discharged from here. Well, hopefully rehab, anyway. Right now, though, it looks like that option's not going to work out."

I had trouble following that, but I wasn't interested. To even bring up discharge plans struck me as premature. That wasn't on my horizon. Anyway, whenever it happened, I knew my wife would handle the details. But, since I was a captive audience, I listened politely.

"My preference is you go straight to an acute rehab hospital. I have a hospital in mind where I'm director of rehab, which would give you continuity in your therapy program," he enthused. "I'd like to get you in there. We can do you some real good. It's sort of a 'boot camp' for patients like you."

His started pointing in rhythm as he continued. "You'd get PT and OT five times a week. They would work on improving strength and mobility and train you on transferring yourself safely, dealing with transitions. They'll teach strategies for dealing with your ADLs, the activities of daily life."

That's what I wanted, and knew it would be ideal to remain under his care during that phase of my recovery. I nodded in agreement.

"That sounds terrific, Doctor, will they –"

"But . . . " Dr. Barone interrupted. "Based on everything else that's going on, and what Doctor Kumar and Doctor Sinha tell me, the timing is not in your favor. The decision will be based on how strong and mobile you are when all the tubes come out. It would be great if we keep you here, down on the second floor, so you could continue getting therapy until you're ready for rehab. Unfortunately, the HMO probably isn't going to authorize that."

I was listening closely now. Where would I go if not to rehab?

"Which brings us to option two, which looks most likely right now," he continued. He looked regretful. "And that is, you go to a nursing home."

I was startled. That didn't sound like a move forward.

"At the nursing home they'd help you get around between the bed and the chair, they'd feed you, but they don't provide therapy." He shrugged. "You'd have to get stronger and ready for acute rehab on your own, without an organized therapy program.

Even then, there's no guarantee after that. It's possible the HMO will discharge you directly to home with no acute rehab."

I felt threatened. I was angry. If I stop therapy, I could go backwards. All of my muscles and joints were barely active and moving; they needed continued, uninterrupted work. Without professional therapy there was a good chance the joints won't fully loosen and always be limited or locked up, and the unused muscles might atrophy before they get reconnected to my nerves. Even a delay will foreclose my optimal recovery. Yet the HMO was ready to cut me loose regardless of what was best for me.

It was me versus the HMO in a race against time. If I win, I'll get the care I need to achieve the best possible future. If I lose, my only chance to achieve anything like a normal life may be gone forever.

When Dr. Kumar told me that he was going to remove the tracheostomy, I was scared. I didn't think I was ready. I was concerned my breathing capacity would not be sufficient, and was aware there was still a pocket of pleural fluid on the right side of my chest. I hadn't used the ventilator for several days, relying only on the nasal cannula for oxygen, but still clung to the reassurance that I could be reconnected through the tracheostomy if I needed it. I felt uneasy to lose that option. Of course, I deferred to the doctor's judgment, despite my misgivings.

Before he began, I asked him, "If this doesn't work out, could you put it back?"

"The opening does begin to narrow quickly, but if it is done within a few hours, it can be replaced quite easily most of the time.

"I don't anticipate any problem, though," he continued. "You have been breathing on your own for three days with the tracheostomy capped and on oxygen through the nasal prongs. Just relax and breath slowly! You will be fine. I will tell your RT to keep a close eye and call me if there are any difficulties. I won't be far away."

He performed the procedure at bedside during his regular rounds, a little after nine. I was nervous before and remained quite anxious afterward. In theory, without the tube in my airway it should have been easier to breathe, but I felt no improvement and was very uncomfortable.

By the end of the second hour, my difficulties grew worse. I couldn't get a satisfying breath, and I tossed and turned and sat the bed up higher, hoping to open up my lungs. These feelings and actions brought back troubling memories of what I went through before I stopped breathing. I tried to relax, breathe slowly, and inhale deeply. Instead, my inhalations grew shallower, which increased my stress. I started gasping for air, and then the horrible squeezing feeling of suffocation closed around my chest.

I lost control. My shoulders started bucking and I began to hyperventilate, gulping for air with no capacity for it. Spasms overtook my body. As I felt this cycle of futility spinning me down, I managed to reach the call button.

"Slow down! Slow down your breathing, Mr. Walsh," urged the RT when she arrived. I could not, and every muscle in my body clenched. My heart was hammering inside my chest, and panic seized my mind. *After all this time, I can still die from this!*

She had already slipped a mask with a bag attached over my face, and within a few moments each shuddering breath came a split-second later than the previous one. Minutes later I was resting, an oxygen cannula under my nose, my pulse rate and blood pressure moderating. My oxygen saturation was back in the mid-nineties after falling to only eighty-five percent in the midst of the attack.

My big moment had become a fiasco. I was embarrassed to have done so poorly. I was disgusted by my weakness. I felt ashamed, believing I must have panicked like when I first tried CPAP. This failure, after failing the motility test a few days before, made me question whether I was trying my best.

My emotions crashed. I felt bitter, as I had many times, but now toward myself, remorseful for being a burden. I could sense my wife and daughter were wearing out. I felt I was letting down my entire team by not getting better faster. I obsessed on the fact I caused this entire calamity myself by ingesting the *C. botulinum* spores. A sense of intense guilt began burning in the back of my mind.

Dr. Kumar replaced the tracheostomy early in the afternoon. He explained I was fortunate, in a way.

"The hole was closing quickly. It was so narrow I had to use the smallest size they make, George. If this crisis happened a few days from now, after the opening was smaller or if it had closed, it would have been necessary to intubate you through the oral cavity, as you were the very first time, followed by putting in a new tracheostomy."

That was small consolation for how badly I felt. I believed my panic was a mental failing and this was all my fault.

The beat-up armchair probably hadn't moved from this room since the hospital opened back in the 1960s. The wood frame was battered and greasy, the blue fabric was worn and stained, a corner of the seat cushion was missing. Whenever Dr. Kumar pulled it over and sat down at the side of the bed, as he did that morning, I knew it was going to be an important conversation.

He greeted my wife, who sat silhouetted against the white cabinets. He was on my right, lit by the diffused glow from the window and wearing a crisp white lab coat, starched blue shirt, and diagonal striped tie. Framed by the open door, he was the image of calm while the constant activity of the nurses' station swirled behind him.

He was frowning. "You are making considerable progress in many ways," he said, "but there are two issues we need to address.

"The first is your digestion. Your intestinal motility has barely improved. Doctor Sinha and I can only detect occasional bowel sounds. Considering where you are in your walking and motor skills, you should be much farther along.

"The crux of the problem, as I see it, George, is the pain medication. Narcotics like Dilaudid can reduce or stop motility. It also suppresses respiration. I am sure it was a factor the other day when you could not tolerate the tracheostomy removal.

"Several months ago, you agreed that you would taper off. I see you are using less lately, but yesterday you asked for four shots."

I glanced at my wife. Her face was turned toward Dr. Kumar, but her eyebrows shot up. I quickly looked back at him so our eyes would not meet.

"Only you know your level of pain," the doctor continued, "but I believe this is the time to consider discontinuing the Dilaudid. Doctor Barone will also taper off the fentanyl if you agree. But it is your decision."

His gaze was steady. I sensed he trusted me to make the right choice to advance my recovery. I didn't want to let him down, but I was on the spot – I wanted another shot. I looked away.

As had been true since mid-summer, I didn't need it for pain anymore. I used it for recreation, to kill time. I justified it as my treat for being sick, it was my only fun when I couldn't even eat. And I told myself I had it under control.

I didn't do any in the morning in order to have the most energy and better focus in therapy, to put in the best effort and reap the greatest benefit. Around noon I grew bored and got a shot. Then another afternoon shot, which I tried to get before my wife came in to hide from her how much I was using. I'd ask for another soon after she left at night, or at my first awakening. Then I'd get one more before the morning change of shift. I rationalized that the night shots didn't count because they helped me doze off, and I did need the rest. But in reality, it was all about the buzz, not the sleep.

Yet, it hadn't been fun for a long time. Dilaudid no longer

offered a blessed escape, only a headache and slight nausea after a few minutes of mild distraction. But I kept asking for it. I knew I was addicted. In fact, I was already thinking of my next shot when the doctor came in. Can I ask him to stop it tomorrow, or after just one more? That would be embarrassing, but for a split second I considered negotiating to put off the inevitable.

I had to admit the truth. I had been angry with myself for failing the motility X-ray and the trach removal attempt, and I now understood my addiction set me up for those failures.

I was at a fork in the road. In front of me was the opportunity to stop using, to address my guilty feelings, correct the problem, and move forward. All I needed was a few seconds of strength to put the issue behind me. If I could find the breath to say the words, the struggle still raging inside me would be over.

I glanced at my wife; she was looking at me with – was it hope, a plea? I didn't want to let the doctor down, but I couldn't let her down.

I turned toward Dr. Kumar and waved my hand. "Let's DC it," I said, using the abbreviation for "discontinue."

His expression did not change. He nodded and said, "I will put in the order."

I looked back at my wife. I thought she showed a look of satisfaction mixed with surprise. I wondered if she was proud of me, thinking I was courageous or strong or something admirable. I was none of those. I was just smart enough to say "stop" when the doctor offered an easy way out.

"The second issue is the pleural effusion," Dr. Kumar continued, "the pocket of excess fluid on the right side of your chest. It did not get absorbed and decrease as I had been expecting all along. It did not seem large enough to remove it until now, and when you were on the ventilator it was not worth the risk. Now the amount seems sufficient to remove it, which should improve your lung capacity. This is done by a procedure called thoracentesis. In this I will insert a catheter into the chest cavity to drain the fluid."

"Is this lung surgery?" I was afraid, worried I was too frail for an operation.

"Oh, no, no," the doctor reassured me. "It is performed at bedside, with a local anesthetic. To prevent damage to the lung, we use ultrasound to guide the placement of the needle."

He paused. "I would like to do it tomorrow afternoon."

"I, I can make that," I said, distracted by the word "needle."

The next day, around three, the ultrasound tech brought in his machine and began setting up. A nurse arrived and laid out the instruments and prep kit for the procedure. Then she brought the patient table over to the left side of the bed. Just when she was positioning me leaning over it, Dr. Kumar walked in.

He was calm and businesslike. Speaking softly, he gave his

instructions to the nurse and tech as they got to work.

I felt the cold ultrasound gel on my back and the pressure of the scanning head moving over my ribs, going back and forth, then lingering at one place before pulling away. I felt the technician mark an "X" on the spot. Then came the coolness of antiseptic wiped on my skin, circling around and around.

"You will feel a pinch, George." I felt the little stings as Dr. Kumar administered the local in several places. "You will feel some pressure." I did; it seemed the doctor was pushing his thumb against my back, rather than a needle into it.

After a few uneventful minutes I was tapped out, and he withdrew the catheter. The nurse removed the draping and dressed the wound, then came around the bed to pull away the table I was leaning on. I anticipated a moderate increase in capacity once I straightened.

I sat upright, lifting my shoulders and at the same time taking in a breath. My eyes popped open at the sensation of my entire chest filling with air – including the formerly empty space deep in my lower right lung. I felt a sudden expansion of my chest above the diaphragm when the first rush of air filled me all the way down. It was invigorating and liberating after so many months of living with the primal fear of suffocation.

Dr. Kumar drew out of me just over 800cc of a rather dark yellow fluid – which equals approximately 24 ounces, more than a typical bottle of wine or a medium soda at a fast-food restaurant. Visualize that much space – now take a breath yourself and imagine how great it felt to have that much capacity restored to me.

I was excited. My entire body felt better. I had more energy, even lying in bed. With this change, I knew I could put up more sail and hoped to catch a freshening wind to speed me on the next leg of my journey.

My withdrawal from the pain killers was much easier than I feared it would be. One factor was that the improvements and changes occurring at the time forced me to move forward. Another, surprising to me, was that temptation wasn't an issue. Knowing it was out of reach helped push it out of mind. There was no chance of backsliding; Dr. Kumar wasn't going to change his mind and I couldn't sneak away and buy some. Also, I was angry with myself and felt guilty. I saw how addiction slowed down my recovery and may have cost me the chance of getting into acute rehab. A quick rush with a few minutes of distraction, followed by headache and queasiness, wasn't worth that loss.

Almost before I noticed I had missed a few shots, on the day after the thoracentesis, they removed the Foley catheter – and didn't put in another. It was a relief to be free of the constant invasive discomfort after nine months, and the loss of privacy. I had accepted it as necessary; you don't dwell on it. Yet it was stressful, both having one and worrying whether I'd function normally when it was removed, or if the muscles had atrophied during the long paralysis.

I prepared for this with bladder training. It starts by closing off the valve on the collector tube, causing the flow to back up and build up pressure inside the bladder. That was supposed to let me regain sensation, and flexing the bladder would reconnect the muscles by stretching and working them, like therapy on every other part of me. When the moment of truth arrived, the training proved successful. I had sufficient control although little capacity, but it was a start.

Unfortunately, it was also a difficult maneuver to perform in bed, and often messy. My hands had trouble gripping the urinal, my reclining posture was awkward for the task, and I couldn't roll onto my side. I also had to do it frequently, which at least distracted me from thinking about the pain shots.

I was happy to take this step, but the challenge of dealing with it and avoiding the inevitable messes made me determined to get mobile as soon as possible.

Of all the factors that helped me leave addiction behind, the most important was the emotional and physical lift I got after the thoracentesis.

Since my life-and-death crisis, I suffered from low lung capacity. I felt continual shortness of breath and sometimes the distress was acute. In the early months, I often thought I was near suffocation when I was being moved or turned. Now, a great weight had been lifted from my chest. I was no longer afraid it might drag me under and drown me. I was almost giddy to be free of this haunting fear of death.

With the large increase in my oxygen intake I had more energy to pour into therapy – just when I was motivated to do all I can, while I can. My endurance improved immediately; on the first walk after the procedure I matched my previous best distance, and only needed one rest instead of three. I decided to use my new energy to get as much PT as I could before going to the nursing home, and exert myself as much as possible. Athletes say they want to leave it all on the court; I wanted to leave it all in the corridor.

The third or fourth day after the thoracentesis, Kate was the PT for my morning walk. She helped me transfer to the wheelchair, then rolled me out to the hall and up to the walker. Taking a deep breath and with gritted teeth, I placed one hand on the wheelchair arm and the other on the walker – and stood up on my own. Two days earlier, I did not have the strength or energy to do that.

I paused to gather myself. I felt the strange hollowness in my left leg and an intense tingling low in both legs. The tingling started two weeks earlier and was getting worse. I decided it was time I mention it to someone.

"Hey, Kate, every time I stand, the left leg doesn't feel like it's all there. It's like the bone feels numb but not the outside? And both legs have a tingling, especially lower down in the feet and ankles."

She began nodding quickly with a serene smile. It appeared she heard this before, and knew how to deal with it.

"Sometimes it's quite intense. It's worse on the left," I added. I raised my eyebrows, waiting to hear the detailed medical explanation she seemed eager to share.

Her blue eyes twinkled behind her hipster frames. Head still bobbing, she said, "Yeah. That gets better. Now, let's start with your right foot . . . ."

I was exasperated, but realized she was telling me to not get bogged down, to keep looking forward. In a way, she was making my mind skip ahead to the future, and there, this problem will be gone.

Well, okay then, I thought, still frustrated. *Good to know.*

I started my walk. I had been looking forward to this session in particular; I wanted to set a new record. I planned to make a complete lap around our section of the floor, even going past the elevator lobby for the first time, which would take me within a few steps of the doors to the ICU.

On previous walks, I could see them from down the hall, heavy double doors, always closed, of light-colored wood with small square windows. This time, as I approached them more closely than ever, and came near to where I must turn left into another hallway as planned or go straight toward those doors, I was gripped by a powerful curiosity to see my old room.

In all the time I spent there, I never saw it. I knew access to the unit was restricted and I wouldn't be allowed past those doors. But, would they let me just peek inside the ICU, through those little windows? Can I steal one glimpse I can attach to the memories of that dark chapter – and see myself as I was back then, lying on that bed, paralyzed and silent but listening, thinking, waiting?

I knew what Kate would say, if I asked her. With a smirk or a shrug or a laugh, tossing her sandy-colored hair, she'd answer, "Why look back? You want to go forward, right? Right?"

The temptation remained only that. I didn't break stride. I stayed on my path and left behind a part of my life that will always be invisible to me.

My next hurdle was passing the second intestinal motility X-ray. I was eager to get past it but concerned I hadn't had enough time to get ready. Walking was the best exercise for activating my intestines after quitting pain meds, and though I challenged myself to do as much as possible, I only had eight days before the exam was scheduled.

I was confident my intestines had improved, but I decided I also needed a game plan to help me pass. I thought of Rachel's instructions on how to swallow, with deliberation and force.

Based on that idea, this time I was determined to eat with more energy and keep up the pace until I finished the entire appalling egg salad-and-contrast sandwich. My theory was that forcing down more food in less time would make the intestines react with more movement. If true, the last tasteless, texture-less bites would push the first bites farther along, and it will look good on the X-ray.

I carried out the plan and ate the whole dreadful sandwich, despite a dry mouth and without water. Unfortunately, the results showed improved function, but I was not yet normal. It was not safe for me to eat. Dr. Kumar was sorry; I was still NPO.

Frustrated, I tried to make him change his mind. I begged him to let me sip some water to relieve my parched mouth. I pointed out I was so close to passing, certainly, a few sips couldn't hurt. Surely, I can absorb that much. Even that little bit, I suggested, might stimulate motility. I argued the trend was improving, which was true – several signs and measurements indicated digestion was speeding up – so let's be proactive.

It wasn't until four or five days later when the doctor allowed me to have something – ice chips. It was a memory shock; I forgot how cold ice is. I was hypnotized by the frigid material moving down the center of my chest like a narrow avalanche and spreading across my middle, the first sensations inside my digestive tract since early spring. My stomach was so empty, I devoured the entire small cup they brought me but then felt bloated. It was odd to feel full again. I realized my stomach must have shrunk quite a lot to get filled by so little.

Just as I hoped, this tiny bit of intake did increase motility enough that Dr. Kumar was convinced I could eat safely. On his rounds on December 23, he informed me I'd get something for dinner that evening.

A little past five, I heard the familiar wobbling wheels of the food cart that never stopped at my room. This time it did; a moment later the door opened, and the aide came in. She wore a questioning look and was staring down at a piece of paper in one hand while holding something I couldn't see in the other. I imagined that after all this time, she was surprised to be bringing an order to this room.

She looked apologetic, as if she thought she might be bothering me.

"316?"

"Yes, 316."

She handed me a small carton of yogurt along with a cellophane package of plastic utensils and a napkin.

"G'night," she said. She turned away.

I called after her, "Thanks!"

I was eager to dig in but found eating wasn't as simple as I expected. I couldn't tear the cellophane on the utensils even using my teeth. I could barely grip the tab on the yogurt cup's foil cover and could not budge it to peel it open. I needed help to get started. Then, because of my gnarled fingers, the only way I could hold the spoon was to pinch it between my thumb and finger, making it stick out sideways from my fist. To eat, I'd have to scoop out the yogurt like an infant or chimpanzee would.

I looked at the label: strawberry-banana. That sounded good. Then I put the first spoonful in my mouth. It was terrible. I couldn't detect any fruit flavor, and it was quite bitter in spite of being a popular sweetened brand.

It was obvious my taste buds had been switched off by the disease, like my salivary glands and my sense of smell had been. I realized that even if this yogurt was my favorite fettucine or a juicy steak, I wouldn't have tasted or enjoyed that either.

I hoped it wasn't much longer until I could eat and taste regular food again, but was still worried I'd have bowel problems when I did. Only then would I know whether this lengthy paralysis had helped my intestines, or if my Crohn's has been active and is lying in wait for me.

It's not easy spending a big holiday or your birthday in the hospital, and even worse to miss your birthday and many holidays and entire months and several seasons too, as I had by this point. But no matter how long the stay, for most patients, by far the worst time to be stuck in this stressful hospital environment – probably dealing with a serious medical issue or they wouldn't be here at this time – is Christmas.

My holiday party was a gathering I knew I'd always cherish. It was Christmas Eve, and my wife and I and both our children were together in the same place for the first time since before I became paralyzed. It was the first time I was with both my children since I was wheeled away in a gurney to the room where in less than twenty-four hours my life was going to change forever.

A special joy was my son was there, one of his rare visits since the day he got me to the hospital. It wasn't because he didn't want to see me more often, or his mother and sister kept him away so he'd not upset the very tight ship they were running. It was because, just after I was struck down, he got a good job two hours away from our home, two and a half from this hospital, but only five minutes from his son. I think he did the right thing.

I was delighted we were all gathered. But in the selfie we took that evening, I look only mildly pleased. My facial muscles were still very stiff from the paralysis and hadn't moved very much to activate them, as my arms and legs had. It's too bad I could not show how happy I was, but that neutral expression more accurately depicts the mixed emotions that were surging through me.

Along with my great joy, I felt a sharp pang of regret I could not remember the last time all of us were together. I knew it was more recent than the last Christmas but longer than nine months ago, when I went to the ER in late March. My issue wasn't how long ago it was, or that I was sorry I forgot the date or occasion. It troubled me that, at the time, I did not appreciate how precious those moments were. I thought that day was uneventful, but it could have been our last as a family!

A million memories flew through my mind. I shook my head and tried to just take in the moment. I lay back and enjoyed the warm feeling of being with them and listening to their chatter buzzing around me. Yet, I had to wonder, *What can I offer them now?*

I presumed I'd never work again. So, not money. The kids didn't need a taxi driver or a school volunteer anymore. I may not be able to keep up the house or do any improvements. But I realized it was still my purpose in life to help my family any way I could, and I rededicated myself to do so. Even if it's only giving advice or encouragement, I promised I would tackle the job like it might be the last thing on earth I ever do. Because it might.

The thoracentesis improved my breathing so much, Dr. Kumar capped the trach again about two days before the holiday. I was on room air from that day forward, and felt very comfortable and had plenty of energy. I also started exercising on the recumbent bicycle in the therapy department's small gym. It looked like whenever the doctor decided to remove the tracheostomy, this time it would be an easy success. I anticipated passing that milestone early the next week, just before New Year's.

The day of the final trach capping was also the day I got that first cup of yogurt. Within two days I was getting three "meals" a day of a carton of yogurt and a protein drink, plus some clear soup and ice cream. Tube feeding was cut back to only at night. They expected I could completely sustain myself in the normal way within a few days, and Dr. Sinha would take out the G-J tube.

But for me to affect a smooth transition to normal function, especially on such a crucial process, would not be true to my established pattern. Instead, the two steps forward of eating by mouth was followed by one big step back when several intersecting intestinal problems created a crisis on Sunday morning.

I was feeling very good Saturday, but on Sunday I woke up bloated and had a sharp pain across my upper abdomen, under the ribs. That is where I most hated to feel pain. It stirred up frightening memories of my desperate fight with Crohn's. I feared I'd now discover I have a serious problem down there.

My digestive system had come to a dead stop. I had no appetite. I was constipated. I did not absorb any of the overnight tube feeding, which caused the bloating. The pressure made me nauseated. I needed to be medicated to keep from vomiting. Vomit was a serious hazard: it was almost certain I would aspirate it, and my cough was still too weak to clear the airway.

The big question was, is this a temporary pause or a sign of an ileus, an obstruction caused by Crohn's that had been active all along? If it was an obstruction, I'd need urgent surgery in my frail and malnourished condition. The danger and stress of a major operation would make my current situation feel like a picnic.

I spent all day in pain, hoping the odds would break my way. That evening, I needed a powerful sleep aid to get any rest at all.

I awoke in the quiet of the night feeling more comfortable. I was no longer nauseated. I took these as good signs but was still worried. I concentrated on breathing deeply and relaxing my guts, telling myself: *Come on, guys, c'mon! You were fixed up by Dr. Miles himself. Show 'em what a great job he did!*

Dr. Kumar scheduled an X-ray early Monday to rule out a blockage. By late morning, the news I hoped for was confirmed: no obstruction. By mid-afternoon my intestines were moving again. My hunger returned in time for me to have my usual dinner. It had been a terrible scare, but I was back on track.

After this crisis, Dr. Sinha decided to wait until after New Year's to reevaluate the situation. Since he was going to be out of town for a few days after that, this would be no earlier than the following Thursday, a week from New Year's Day. By that time, he reasoned, I'd be fine. Following Dr. Sinha's decision, Dr. Kumar thought it best to leave the tracheostomy in place as well. That way, if I had another such problem and aspirated vomit, the RT would have easy access to clear the airway.

I was relieved motility had resumed, but disappointed to be still stuck in this frustrating pattern and that my progress was further delayed.

On the Tuesday after New Year's, Dr. Kumar came back after completing his rounds to take out the tracheostomy, again. It was no ceremony, although I did recognize it was the end of a long siege. I had been intubated for over nine months. Before he began, the doctor cautioned me, but with a gleam in his eye as if he expected I would do just fine.

"Now remember, George. This time I can't put it back."

"**G**ood morning, Mr. Walsh, how's it going," Dr. Barone asked in his usual descending greeting on his Thursday rounds, one week into the new year.

"I'm doing okay, Doctor," I replied.

I noticed that he, on the other hand, didn't look well. He had taken a lot of time off during the last two months, and my eyes had cleared enough to see he was ill. His walk was more like a shuffle. His face was pale and his eyes puffy behind the thick glass in his heavy, black frames. I noticed the scuff mark on his belt showing he now wore it two notches smaller. I was concerned for him and felt the irony that even the healer is not immune to human frailty.

He got straight to his point in his characteristic indirect manner, his right hand making loose circles in the air while he spoke.

"Well, I guess these extra two weeks made the difference," he said with a chuckle. I didn't understand. "The case manager is working out the details to make sure they'll have a bed. But it looks like it's going to work out, might take a few days, give or take, and then we can transfer you into the rehab facility."

I merely nodded as he went on, with an "uh-huh" or two, and an "I'm . . . not sure" thrown in.

"Good. Alright," I said.

Then I realized the doctor was talking about acute rehab. My next stop would be the acute rehab hospital, not a nursing home.

"Oh! That's terrific, Doc! Wow, that's great news."

I was surprised and relieved, amazed I finally beat the HMO for once. It was a big win for an invaluable prize: the chance to achieve my best recovery. I didn't think it was possible. I was having trouble believing it was true and felt a little disoriented.

I blew out a long breath. This meant, I figured, I would be here only a few more weeks. "When do you expect that'll happen, Doctor?"

He shrugged. "Oh, about the middle of the week. Probably next Wednesday."

I was already bewildered, but learning *"that day"* I've been waiting for is *"next Wednesday"* stunned me.

I felt almost numb. I glanced around the room, which was so familiar to me: the cabinets, the broken sink, the featureless clock, the blurry television. It occurred to me that all of these things were just images to me; I could never go over and touch them. This aspect of my existence always made the entire experience partly unreal, as if all of it was only happening in my mind. Knowing that in just a few days I would not be seeing any of this, it seemed these sights were already memories. It was a strange, disembodied feeling.

Then I remembered Dr. Barone had said something else.

"What did you mean about the 'two weeks'?" I asked.

He grinned. "Well, if your digestion hadn't stopped on – what was that, the previous Sunday, eleven, twelve days ago? – Dr.

Sinha said he would have removed the G-J that Tuesday. And Dr. Kumar was only waiting for that to happen before he removed the trach. So, yeah. If your intestines had started up smoothly, you would have been transferred to the nursing home last Wednesday afternoon or evening. Your first day up there would have been a week ago today, New Year's Day.

"But, since you were here, we didn't stop your therapy. And, ah, even though you're still sort of on the bubble," he smiled and rocked his hand in the air, palm down, "after these extra two weeks of therapy, especially the PT, you're ready for acute rehab."

I was too astonished to get excited. I was first struck by the irony. I barely won the race and only just qualified for acute rehab – thanks to my "one step forward, two steps back" pattern of recovery that had been so frustrating. The delay caused by the digestive problem gave me more time for therapy. What had appeared to be another setback turned out to be a lucky break.

I was glad but knew acute rehab would be a lot of work. I wondered if I could handle it.

"Am I capable of that?"

Dr. Barone waved his hand. "Oh, yeah. You're doing really well the last two weeks, and it's the best place to continue your forward momentum. The main focus now is to keep the physical rehab going." He was showing much more energy than I saw in him earlier. He was gesturing with both hands, and spoke with more enthusiasm as he went on.

"You still need work on range of motion, and they'll teach you various transfers you'll need to master, using a shower bench, and a lot of walking. They've got a full gym there for more PT exercises than we can do here. We'll get you on the recumbent bike and treadmill so you can build up your strength and wind. Your core. We can work on your balance, negotiating curbs, stairs. We've got some really good OT people there, too.

"I think I told you it's sort of a 'boot camp' for patients like you, where you can get the concentrated therapy you need. You'll get therapy five days a week instead of the two or three here, so you're going to make much faster progress. No question, it's the best place for you."

I could tell he was in his element despite the haze of illness around him. This was his specialty, and he was ready to take the helm for the next leg of my journey. I trusted him, and his passion gave me confidence this was the right course.

"Okay, Doc. Next week, huh? Wow." My mind was still reeling, knowing *that day* was around the corner.

I understood the next step would be demanding, but that didn't faze me. I wanted it to be tough. I wondered how much time it would take; could I do it in two months, three?

"So, how long do you think I'll be there?" I asked. I braced myself for the sentencing, hoping it wouldn't be more than a few additional months.

"I got you authorization for two weeks. You'll be home before the end of this month."

Before I could take in another breath, my world turned upside down, and a thousand loose pieces of understanding and knowledge about my situation tumbled over and fell into a new configuration. My conception of time, my appreciation of my condition, and my vision of my place in the world changed in a fundamental way.

I was a cork in the ocean bobbing on the waves suddenly caught in a mighty current, gaining speed and heading toward shore. I had been cut off from the flow of time, but was now in a rushing flood that would soon land me on that distant coast Dr. Kumar assured me I'd reach.

I knew the shore would be rocky when I washed up. Two weeks of rehab was not long enough to make our life immediately after my homecoming very easy. But that is where I'd be and where I must start rebuilding my life.

The first change I noticed is how I perceived my body and its limitations in relation to carrying out the activities of daily life. I understood how weak I was and that in two weeks I'd still be barely capable of – anything, I supposed. The difficulty and danger of being left on my own for hours each day was obvious. I saw myself hunkering down inside the house and not moving around much.

Before I could think of all the details – getting out of bed by myself; navigating the house; using the bathroom; bending, twisting and reaching to put on clothes; having the grip and shoulder rotation to turn a doorknob – I understood how much of my rehabilitation was going to rely on my own effort, in private, outside the medical environment where I always placed it. It was going to go on over a very long time, and it will take years, a lifestyle of recovery.

It struck me as ironic that I was just barely getting on my feet, the tracheostomy had been out only two days, they're pushing me out on the street in about twenty days, and this means I'm well. I was wrecked, but I wasn't sick. Physically, they had brought me to the minimal level of "better" I was promised. I thought about what lay ahead.

I won't be up on the third floor of a hospital attended by round-the-clock staff, where the lights are always on. I won't be watching dozens of strangers pass by my door every day nor envy them their normal lives, their commutes, errands, eating at home. There will be no doctors and therapists and nurses and aides and housekeepers walking in whenever they wanted.

I'll be alone inside a modest single-story home on a quiet street. I'll sleep in the dark. There will be windows, and I'll be able to look out and see mundane things such as the yard and fence, the trees and sky, birds, sunsets.

I'll be dependent on my wife; I'm going to need a lot of help at first. I'll have to work hard and get self-sufficient in daily life as soon as I can. I don't want to be a burden. In a way, she's getting out of the hospital too. She deserves relief and rest. I mustn't make her go from advocate to nurse.

At least the driving will be over, for both her and our daughter – and now my daughter can concentrate on her own life as a young adult pursuing a career.

Thinking of how lovingly and bravely those two protected me made me choke up a little. I stared at Dr. Barone smiling at me. I sensed satisfaction and pride radiating from him, and I felt a swell of gratitude, to him, my family, Dr. Kumar, and this entire amazing system that brought me to the crest of going home.

I finally took a breath.

"This month? That's great, Doc. Incredible."

"Linda in case management has a call into your wife to see her next time she's in to sign the paperwork, so that's all, y'know, in their hands." He waved his arm dismissively. "Depending on how soon it happens, if I don't see you here before you're transferred, I'll see you there next Thursday. Have a great day, Mr. Walsh."

"You too, Doctor Barone. Thanks. Thank you."

My head fell back on the pillow. I stared straight ahead at the wall that had filled my vision since I first opened my eyes again.

"Incredible," I whispered.

I turned toward the wall on my left, where my wife had taped a photo of my grandson and me, taken just before I got sick. *He's had a birthday since then,* I realized. I wondered what he looked like now, how much had he grown? I stared at it, and, for the first time since they were closed by paralysis and despite being so dry since they opened, my eyes filled with tears.

My last week in that hospital flew by.

The same day Dr. Barone told me the big news, I had my regular OT session with Laurie. As always, she urged me to work harder, do an extra set, and "finish strong." I completed the last set and laid the four-pound bar across my legs.

Laurie was sitting on my left with the white cabinets behind her. Through calm green eyes, she looked at me with a satisfied smile.

"This is the last time we're going to work together, Geo. You've worked hard. Good job!"

I appreciated the compliment, but knew it was her guidance that had brought me this far.

I noticed her eyes narrowed, and her usual tone of friendly challenge turned more serious.

"But, hey, when you're out on your own, do me a favor?"

"Name it," I replied.

"Push yourself."

I knew exactly what she meant. This wasn't a pep talk. This was a continuation of our first meeting. Then, she told me movement would stimulate the growth of new nerve-muscle connections. Today, she was telling me there was a lot of untapped improvement still inside me, and I could develop it by working hard – by pushing myself. Just like at our initial session, she was expanding the horizons of my recovery.

I took her words to heart. I wanted to regain everything I possibly, physically could. *Someone has to have the best recovery from something like this*, I thought. Inspired by her words, I dared to wonder, *Why not me?*

"I will," I promised her, and myself.

By mid-day, the doctor's orders came through, and the IV line was taken out. The IV stand that had loomed over me for so long was rolled away, the pumps' cyan displays now dark. A CNA peeled the telemetry stickers off my chest, but it still itched. I imagined how great it would feel to shower again.

Around five o'clock, Dr. Sinha stopped in to remove the G-J tube. He pulled it out at bedside; it took just a few seconds and that was that – for the first time since my Code Blue I had not a single tube in me. It struck me that on a floor of exclusively ICU and monitored patients, despite being so weak and frail, I was probably the healthiest inmate.

A few days later, Dr. Kumar stopped in on his usual Sunday morning rounds. I didn't expect a visit, since I was no longer getting any medical treatment.

"Good morning, George. I don't wish to bother you, but I have to see you. Although there is no medical reason for me to be here, state law requires it," he said with a gentle smile.

Of course, it was no bother; I was always happy to see him, and he hadn't been in since Dr. Barone told me about my transfer. He pulled the ancient, battered side chair from the corner and sat alongside me facing the television, sitting where the IV pole and respirator had always been.

"Is this the Pittsburgh game? I saw some of this earlier with another patient. Ah, Baltimore has scored since then." He shifted in his chair and looked toward me.

"George, I won't be seeing you again before you leave. I am going back east tomorrow. I am so sorry I won't be here to discharge you myself."

"Yes, that's too bad. Are you going to a medical conference?"

"No, my wife and I are going to see family." He smiled; apparently, he was looking forward to the trip. "They came out a few months ago to stay with us, and now they are reciprocating."

"Nice," I replied. I thought it funny to hear this random detail about his private life, like we were any two friends watching the game and talking.

He asked after my wife and daughter. He was low key; he wasn't going to make a speech or sum up this long journey. At a commercial break he got up, pushed the chair aside, and turned to shake my hand. His hand was thin and strong; I held on to it with both of mine.

"I am glad you are continuing under the care of Dr. Barone. You're in good hands. They are very good over there," he said. He gave me a warm smile, and I again sensed his deep compassion.

"Good luck, George. Give my best to your family. Come back to see us."

I looked in his eyes. "Can I tell you a story?"

"Certainly," he replied. I released his hand.

"It's about the first time we met," I began. I briefly described what I experienced that afternoon, his ominous silence, how I thought he was wearing a mask, my anxiety when he came over to the respirator. I quoted his own words to him, introducing himself and telling me that I absolutely will get better.

"Doctor, in all that time, you were the first person to tell me I'd get better. It was the first time I had any hope at all. That made everything else possible."

He looked at me, shaking his head. "I don't remember."

"I'll never forget," I insisted. "That was the turning point."

The next morning, Marielle was in a sunny mood when she and Deborah arrived with the wheelchair and walker.

"Okay, Mr. Walsh! We get to go for your walk. One . . . last . . . time!" she sang out. She clasped her hands over her heart. "Before they transfer you! Oh, you must be so excited!"

I could now walk more than two full loops around the floor. Sometimes I didn't need to sit to catch my breath, but could just pause and remain standing. On the second loop, passing by the walk-on scale, I asked to stop and check my weight. Marielle and Deborah helped me turn from the walker and step onto the black rubber mat. I was wobbly and had a weak grip on the handles; I felt a hand at my lower back to steady me. I looked down at the digital display. A row of red dashes flashed a few times, and the numbers appeared.

One hundred fourteen point nine.

Before my Crohn's flared up, I weighed close to two hundred pounds. I had lost almost eighty-five pounds in the intervening three years, over forty percent of my body weight. It was hard to believe I could lose so much and still be alive, but that was the fact staring me in the face.

On Wednesday, a woman from the office came up and informed me they were transferring me that night. At noon, another woman asked me to give up the room so they can get it ready for a new patient. This time, after five or six previous refusals, I agreed. Within the hour I left "the lucky room" – I always wanted to walk out of there but still needed a wheelchair – said goodbye to the staff on duty, got several very big hugs, and was taken down to the second floor. I expected I could tolerate being parked in a double room for a few hours.

I was pleasantly surprised when they took me to a single-bed room. It was also all the way down the hall in a corner of the floor, far from the nurses' station, the slamming doors, the constant noise, the foot traffic. It was calm and restful and, making it even more of a change from the grim cell I had occupied, in this room the bathroom was along the corridor side, where it should be. That meant I could see out a bank of windows stretching across the entire exterior wall.

I lay there in peace and looked out at a row of sturdy eucalyptus extending away from the hospital. I watched the shimmering display of gentle breezes tossing the trees' dusty green leaves, flashing their silver undersides. When I came into this place I was frightened by the wind; on this afternoon, I knew it was inviting me home.

With the approach of evening, the golden glow of a coastal

California sunset lit the scene with a glorious light. I stared, trying to not even blink so I wouldn't miss a second of its beauty.

In time, I heard the clatter of a gurney, and then the voices of the transport team and a nurse coming down the hall and into the room. They transferred me to the gurney, strapped me down, and wheeled me out the same automatic double doors I passed through when I came here – totally locked-in – nine months earlier, to the very day.

Acute rehabilitation brought about significant improvements in the next fifteen days. I expected it to be hard work, which it was, but I was surprised at the mental adjustment I had to make. It was a complete change of perspective to give up being a passive, maximum-assist patient reliant on others. I went from being a man recovering from catastrophic total paralysis to one preparing for an independent life.

I had been confined in my solitary room for endless months and alone inside my mind for much of that, but here I was eating with a group of fellow swallow risks and talking about just anything. The common room was on the second story and had panoramic windows, so I could see the weather, rooftops, trees. Each morning at breakfast I noted that the sun was a little higher at that time than it was the day before. I could see a few distant office towers and a glimpse of a freeway – I recognized the area and realized I was only blocks from my favorite fettuccini Alfredo. I was on a regular diet of solid food again and knew it wouldn't be long until I'd be eating there.

The gym was well equipped and expanded my PT therapies, which accelerated my progress. It was fun and encouraging to be working alongside other people determined to reach their own goals. Although we each had our own story, we were on the same team. Patients and staff, we were all pulling in the same direction.

My OT, Pamela, finished the work on loosening my left shoulder, so by the second week I could put on a tee shirt. I was also able to transfer from the bed to the walker without help, and from there to the wheelchair. I could get to the bathroom on my own, and look myself in the mirror while brushing my teeth.

I tried stairs, a curb, took a few steps without the walker. I learned to transfer to and use a shower bench – this was critical because I wanted to minimize the need for my wife to help with more physical tasks like this. It was a wonderful feeling to shower again, and to wash my hair. I learned about devices to assist me at home, such as one to help me put on socks, and one to extend my reach and pick things up.

Then the evening came when my wife could take me home.

She came up to the room and gathered my belongings. An aide brought me downstairs in a wheelchair and out to the car. I was able to stand on my own, and then, holding on to the door, turn and lower myself until I plopped down the last several inches into the seat. My wife lifted my feet and swung them into the car, pivoting me like a mannequin, and buckled me in. The seat was wider than I remembered, at least compared to this thin body.

I felt anxious to be sitting in a car, surrounded by glass, out in the open air, under streetlights, instead of being in a bed in a room in a building. This seemed dangerous and wild.

My wife got in the car. She reached over and rubbed my leg. "Are you ready to go home, sweetie?"

"Yeah. Yeah, I want to go home," I blurted, surprised at the urgency in my voice.

She turned the key. The vibrations of the motor flowed upward through me. Within moments we turned onto the freeway ramp and I felt myself sliding toward the door, then pulled back into the seat when she accelerated. We were close to an interchange, and I was dazzled as the tangle of traffic merged and we joined a mighty stream of red lights and dark gleaming metal. To the left, an equally powerful river of white lights surged past us with insistent energy.

I thought how each vehicle was hurrying someone to their particular place, and now I was going to mine.

It wasn't long until we were on our street and pulling into the driveway. The front light was on, showing the same curve of the walkway, the bushes, the wind chime. My wife helped me get up into my walker, and I shuffled along after her. I concentrated on walking safely to the front door and taking the small step up into the house. Inside, I took three or four more steps and stopped. Our dogs ran to me, barking the alarm, but quickly hushed. They acted confused, not sure what to make of this guy.

I gazed at the familiar interior, the carpet and tile, couch and coffee table, lamps, cabinets, pictures. I was shocked to find everything looked the same.

I moved farther inside, and my wife closed the door. She looked at me with relief in her eyes and blew out a sigh. She managed a tired smile and said, "Welcome home, honey."

I stared at her. My mind was spinning. My thoughts leapt back to the morning when she let me know I would not face this alone. I was deluged with memories of all the times she protected me, managed my care, confronted negligent staff, dealt with insurance companies, held my hand for hours and hours through a hospitalization lasting over three hundred days – I was overwhelmed. Here before me was the person most responsible for getting me home, and I had so much to say, to thank her for, to apologize for.

"You . . . ," I began, but I couldn't get past the first word. My throat tightened. My eyes begged her to understand.

She reached out and squeezed my arm. "Come sit down," she whispered. She turned toward the family room.

The dogs followed us and remained vigilant after I eased myself into my chair. My wife sat in hers.

It was hard to believe I was in my own chair instead of a hospital bed. It was strange how quiet it was. I was disoriented taking in all the details. I glanced around the room, straight ahead at the television, down at the carpet pattern, then lifted my head while looking up toward the front window.

I felt a jolt – the memory of that moment when the double vision appeared – the harbinger of a disaster I barely escaped. Thoughts and feelings flooded in of the mortal danger and desperate struggle that followed, and the pain and isolation it foretold. I winced as I recalled that when I went to the ER, I had no conception I would not come home for over ten months, much less that I almost didn't come home. I felt grateful, relieved, humbled, and astounded to have survived such a close brush with death.

I closed my eyes and took a deep breath. I slowly blew it out and savored the silence. I felt exhausted down to my bones.

Suddenly the dogs began barking and ran toward the door. I heard a cheery, "Hello, Walshes!" as our neighbor friend, Kerri, let herself in. Earlier, my wife told her I was coming home that evening, and when she saw us pull up, she decided to check on me. She came to me, leaned over to hug my shoulders, and sat down on the couch.

"Gosh, Geo, we're all so glad you're home. We were so worried." She frowned, looking in my eyes, shaking her head.

"Thank you," I replied.

She tilted her head in a look of curiosity. "God, that was freaky, though! Who'd have thought – botulism? So, it was honey that gave it to you?"

"Yeah, we think so."

"And it was related to the Crohn's you had?"

"I believe so. I'm going to do some research on it."

Her face turned sympathetic again. "So, how are you now?"

"Well, I'm doing okay," I began, and took a deep breath so I could give her the current status, my rehab plan, news on my range of motion, and so forth. But before I could continue, she turned to my wife and started talking about a party she was planning.

At first, I was insulted she cut off my monologue. Then I laughed out loud at my foolishness as I recognized something that was indescribably precious to me.

I was back in the normal world now, and this story was no longer all about, only about, me.

Epilogue

I smiled as the automatic doors swooshed open at my approach. I felt great satisfaction knowing that although I couldn't walk out of this hospital, I was walking back in.

My eyes could focus well, and I had new eyeglasses, so I could see the lobby was smaller than I remembered from the one trip I took outside. I put my packages on the sparkling black countertop and explained my business, showed my ID, signed in, and got a bright yellow visitor's wristband. I looked down at it and laughed. *Yes, I'm only a visitor, now.* I blew out a sigh of astonishment that I could come back here under my own power.

I was just able to press the button for the third floor with my knuckle. My arms were full with two big pink boxes, and the aroma of the three dozen fresh doughnuts, pastries, muffins, and croissants filled the elevator. As it creaked and shook its way upward, I reviewed how my plan for this Tuesday morning in late September was unfolding.

I had kept in touch with Daniel, the RN we befriended. He helped me plan my visit so I could see him again along with as many as possible of the other nurses, LVNs, CNAs, and therapists I wanted to thank in person. But more important, it needed to be a Tuesday morning so I'd be certain to see one particular doctor who would stop in to see me on his rounds at that time on that day.

The elevator shuddered to a stop; the scratched and dented doors rattled open. I took in a deep breath, exhaled, stepped out, and turned left toward the nurses' station and my old room.

I looked down the corridor. It had always been crowded and bustling, but today it was deserted and the nurses' station empty – except for one man standing at the near end of the counter. He was a thin, ramrod-straight figure in a lab coat, dark skinned, with a white goatee and wireless glasses. Hands in his coat pockets, thumbs out, he was calmly looking straight into my eyes as if he knew I was going to step off the elevator that very second.

I approached him, amazed at this uncanny situation. *This is like a scene in a movie,* I thought. *The one person I most want to see is the only person here.* He was coolly appraising me, but his smile showed satisfaction and, I imagined, affection.

"Doctor Kumar, it's great to see you," I said. I put down the boxes and shook his hand with both of mine.

"Hello, George. You look better than the last time we saw you," he replied with a chuckle in his voice.

We were still shaking hands when a nurse and LVN came around a corner talking loudly, another nurse rushed into the station, two CNAs discussing a patient walked up, the housekeeping guy with his cart rolled by, a phone started ringing – and just that quickly the area was back in its normal, chaotic state.

I was mobbed by staff greeting me and asking questions. Within moments, Laurie and Kate arrived.

"Well, look at you!" Kate said with a warm, relaxed smile, scanning me from head to toe.

I had a report to make. "Kate, remember the intense tingling feeling in my legs I complained about that was almost painful? Well, I wasn't sure you knew what I was talking about. But you said that would go away, and it did."

"Well, I told you so!" She laughed, tossing her hair with a one-shoulder shrug.

Laurie had her lower lip out, eyes narrowed, studying me.

"You look like you're doing pretty good, Geo." Her eyes widened. She shook her head. "And considering where you started!" Then her eyes narrowed again. She gave me a nod. I must have passed inspection.

"Laurie, I have to thank you for something." I pointed a crooked finger. "On the last day we worked together, you told me, 'Push yourself.' I want you to know I think of those words every single day. That's been . . . a big help." I was starting to choke up, and felt embarrassed. "It's been really important. Thank you."

She took it in stride and calmly smiled. "Well, good. You're welcome." She reached out and squeezed my upper arm. "Keep going," she urged.

I looked over the crowd and saw Marielle hurrying down the hall, eyes wide open as if anxious to join the reunion. I stepped away from the group into the middle of the hallway. "Hey, Marielle," I called. She glanced up; our eyes met.

"Look at this!" I spread out my arms and balanced on one foot. She burst out laughing, covering her mouth and stomach, and slumped against the corridor wall.

When she recovered, she came over with her arms open and hugged me. Beaming at me, she said, "You're doing so well. We're all so proud of you."

"Hey, there's Doctor B," somebody said. I turned to see Dr. Barone hurrying down the hall. He stopped when he saw the gathering and came up to shake my hand.

"Good morning, Mr. Walsh, how's it going?" he asked in his descending drone. I was happy to see he had good color in his face and appeared to be fine. He was pleased to see I was doing well, but didn't have time to get any details. He could only stop long enough to have our photo taken before he rushed off to see his patient. I was relieved for his sake he was healthy again, and glad he could carry on his work.

Various groups of staffers circulated around the station while I recited my rehearsed status report and answered all their questions. I was astonished at the depth and sincerity of their happiness for my recovery. I had come to thank them, but they seemed happier for me than I did. I didn't expect that, and it stunned me. Right then, I was the beneficiary of such an overabundance of goodwill, I thought I might be experiencing the most joyous moment of my life.

Amid all the glad feelings, I remembered I needed to get a picture with Dr. Kumar before he went back to his patients. I stood next to him and gave my phone to Daniel to take the shot.

I handed it over and said, "This is great, to get a picture of me with my hero."

The doctor leaned back and turned towards me, frowning. He looked into my eyes and pointed for emphasis.

"No," he said. "You are my hero."

I was speechless at his generosity. I smiled, shook his hand, and turned toward the camera. *What a class guy,* I thought.

The next day I was able to navigate two airports and a long flight back to my home town to see my mother, my six siblings, their spouses and kids, and their kids' kids. They held a party in my honor at my brother's family's apartment on the first floor of a classic red brick two-flat, downstairs from my Mom.

With maybe thirty people from four generations in the crowded flat, there were at least sixty conversations going on at any one time. I couldn't pick up all the words, but I loved hearing the music of their voices.

Late in the party I sat with my Mom in the front room. I was on the couch, and she was in an easy chair with the afternoon sun slanting through the blinds behind her. I marveled at all this life swirling around us. I looked at her, her pale blue eyes beaming with pride and love for her family, and thought how happy I was to see that face again. I thought to myself:

How can one man be so lucky?

Acknowledgments

I wish to express special thanks and appreciation to two people who visited me frequently, for their extraordinary caring and encouragement: my sister-in-law PG who came to see me every week I was in acute care but one and helped me keep faith that I had a future, and my friend TE for reading me stories while I was in the dark and helping me remember there was a real world outside my drama.

I also want to thank the cast of characters I encountered in the medical field who brought me through this journey, doctors, nurses, therapists, techs, even one transport driver and a woman who worked in housekeeping who was among the most inspiring people I have ever met, for their dedication to their vocation and their commitment to their patients.

Finally, I thank my family for the greatest gift I have ever received, their love.

Made in the USA
Las Vegas, NV
09 September 2021